RÉSUMÉS
THAT GET
JOBS

RÉSUMÉS THAT GET JOBS

HOW TO WRITE YOUR BEST RÉSUMÉ

by RESUME SERVICE

Jean Reed, editor

ARCO PUBLISHING, INC.
219 PARK AVENUE SOUTH, NEW YORK, N.Y. 10003

Third Edition, Fourth Printing, 1984

Published by Arco Publishing, Inc.
219 Park Avenue South, New York, N.Y. 10003

Copyright © 1981, 1976, 1967, 1963
by Arco Publishing, Inc.

Library of Congress Cataloging in Publication Data
Resume Service.
  Resumes that get jobs.

  1. Resumes (Employment) 2. Applications for
positions. I. Reed, Jean. II. Title.
HF5383.G725   1981   650.1'4   80-26456
ISBN 0-668-05202-3 (Library Edition)
ISBN 0-668-05210-4 (Paper Edition)

Printed in the United States of America

Contents

1
ESSENTIAL INFORMATION

2
SAMPLE RESUMES

3
FOR WOMEN RETURNING TO THE
JOB MARKET

1

Essential Information

About Resumes

WHAT IS A RESUME?

Résumé is a French word meaning "summary"—pronounced REZ-oo-may. Although many dictionaries spell the word with accents (résumé), it is acceptable to drop them as we have in this book.

For the job hunter, a resume containing a "summary" of the pertinent facts about him/herself has become an indispensable tool. A good resume can be the deciding factor in determining whether a prospective employer grants the eagerly sought interview. Through a well-prepared resume, you may literally get "one foot in the door."

A resume has an additional function. *During* the interview a resume serves as a point of reference and an advantageous focal point for conversation between the job-hunter and the prospective employer.

HOW TO MAKE THE BEST USE OF YOUR RESUME

1. An obvious, but limited, use of your resume is to send it where you know an opening exists or in answer to an advertisement. At management level, the *Wall Street Journal*'s "National Business Employment Weekly," a compilation of career-advancement positions from the paper's four regional editions, is an excellent source. It is priced at $2.50 a copy and may be obtained from the National Business Employment Weekly, c/o Dow Jones & Co. Inc., 22 Courtlandt Street, New York, N.Y. 10007.

2. A broader use of your resume is to search out your own openings. We suggest the following:

(a) STATE EMPLOYMENT AGENCIES (newly named "State Employment Security Agencies"). There has been a big push to upgrade state agencies and the quality of job orders. Tax paying employers are beginning to realize that they are paying for these services and more and more are taking advantage of it. Job seekers are the beneficiaries, and it is foolish to ignore these free services that are yours for the asking.

Contact the state agency in your city, listed in the Yellow Pages under "State of...." Or write the United States Department of Labor, Employment and Training Administration, 601 D Street, N. W., Room 3122, Washington, D.C. 20213 and request your free copy of the *Directory of Local Employment Security Offices*. It contains the name, address and phone number of every state employment office in the United States, Hawaii, Puerto Rico, Guam and the Virgin Islands. The *Directory* clearly states that "the employment security agency of each state implements a Federal/State program which provides applicant and employer services to clients needing this assistance." Other suggested uses of the publication include: workers who need or decide to move from one state to another; workers who want to file an interstate unemployment insurance claim; employers who want to locate a new branch in a different state and need help in staffing it.

An additional free service available to the

job seeker is a detailed publication, *Occupations in Demand at Job Service Offices*, giving area demands for specific occupations, salary range and educational requirements. Request it from the Consumer Information Center, Pueblo, Colo. 81009.

(b) CHAMBERS OF COMMERCE. Get their current directories of area businesses (usually around $2.00). Check through for firms and businesses that could logically use your services. Call each one. Get a top person's name and title (letters handed "down" get far more attention than those handed "up"). Using the properly spelled name and exact title, write a covering letter and attach your resume. Keep a copy of your dated letter.

If you have received no reply within ten to fourteen days, call the person to whom you addressed the letter. If you reach the party, refer to your dated letter and ask if you may be permitted to come in and discuss the matter personally. If your contact is "out" or "in conference," write a follow-up letter, referring to your first letter, and politely request a reply.

If there is no response to your second letter, and you are eager for the job or opportunity, show up at the firm and try to talk to someone in authority. Bull-headed persistence and sheer determination are job-hunting virtues. The paralegal resume that appears later in this book is a prime example. An older woman, fresh out of junior college with newly acquired paralegal qualifications, found her letters to the Public Defender's office were being ignored. Stubbornly refusing to give in or up, she marched down to the office, insisted on talking with the Public Defender himself, and talked herself into a three-month probationary job at no salary. She was confident that given the opportunity she could prove herself. She did, and is now a full-time "Investigator" taking sly delight in the Public Defender's pride in his astuteness for having discovered her.

(c) EMPLOYMENT AGENCIES. In many cases, these should be the last resort. They can be expensive as well as non-productive. If you decide to use an agency, check their walls for licensing or some type of certification. Ask tough questions. Find out about fees and insist on getting a firm, exact reply. Ask what their policy is if you quit or get dismissed from the job they find for you. Remember, you are the *buyer* of their services. Don't be intimidated. Demand details and get everything in writing. Watch what you sign. Read the fine print. Read between the lines.

(d) HELP WANTED. These columns are scrutinized by many employment agencies who will call the advertiser and declare "I've got the person for the job." These columns are equally available to you at no charge. Use them. At certain levels they can be productive with a good resume and covering letter.

(e) JOBS WANTED. A well-worded advertisement in the "Jobs Wanted" section of a newspaper is a gamble, at best. However, you can sweeten the odds by carefully selecting the publication in which you place your ad. Your ad will often get lost in a large city newspaper. On the other hand, cities and counties frequently have small, weekly neighborhood newspapers which are devoured by local residents for area news. The classified section is small and your advertisement could be read by an interested executive.

(f) VOCATIONAL SCHOOLS AND COLLEGE PLACEMENT OFFICES. Although most effort is concentrated on graduates, school placement personnel heads are generally friendly and cooperative about divulging openings they are unable to fill, or steering you to ones that are likely to exist.

Skeleton Resume

You are cautioned at the outset to forget everything you have ever read or heard about a resume. While no two people agree on the exact form and content of a resume, there is, nevertheless, a sizable area of full agreement among employers and personnel people. We urge you to stay within these areas. We are, therefore, going to teach you to write the type of resume that will appeal to the people who count—those who will read the resume. The form of the resume that we shall present has been uniformly accepted by employers the nation over as being concise, informative and clear.

You will note that the first page of our resume format is a synopsis (or condensation) of the amplification that follows. This form has a distinct advantage. It enables an employer to tell at a glance whether or not he wants to know more about you. If he likes what he sees in the synopsis, he will be eager to read the amplification which follows. If he does not care for what he has read in the synopsis, you have saved his time and yours.

Following is a skeleton resume to show the basic resume form. It is practical because it is flexible. You will see that infinite variations are possible. For example, if your position is more impressive than the company name, reverse placement of "title" and "company name." However, for sake of appearance, be consistent and follow this procedure for all employments listed. If you have an excellent education, and employment has been part-time or relatively unimportant, reverse the position of "Employment" and "Education." You will have to decide for yourself what is most important to the person who is going to read your resume.

SYNOPSIS PART OF RESUME

Synopsis of Resume of:
John Doe

Street, City, State, Zip Code
Phone: (area code) number

JOB OBJECTIVE

EMPLOYMENT

Dates (start-end) Name of Company, Address of Company.
Present or last   Company line
  company   Job title

Dates (start-end) Name of Company, Address of Company.
                    Company line
                    Job title

Dates (start-end) Name of Company, Address of Company.
                    Company line
                    Job title

MISCELLANEOUS EMPLOYMENT

Grouping of part-time and/or minor employments

EDUCATION

Dates   High School—type of diploma (academic, etc.)
  (start-finish) Note: unnecessary if college is shown.

Dates   College name—location
  (start-finish) Degree: Major: Minor:
                    [Class standing:]*
                    [Honors:]
                    [Expenses: percentage earned]
                    [Activities: extracurricular]
Miscellaneous   Company courses, Correspondence courses,
  Education   Seminars, Home study.

PERSONAL

Age: Day, month, year of birth. [Place of birth.]
Appearance: Height. Weight. Health (good) (excellent)
Marital Status: (married) (single) (divorced) No. of children
Residence: (own) (rent); will or will not relocate.
Hobbies: Optional
Affiliations: Optional, unless job-related.

(FOR AMPLIFICATION PLEASE SEE FOLLOWING)
Items in brackets are optional, depending on position applied for.

AMPLIFICATION PART OF RESUME

Resume of
John Doe

EMPLOYMENT

Date of starting to present
FULL NAME OF LAST OR PRESENT COMPANY

  Responsibilities:

  Results:

  Reason for leaving:

Date of starting to date of leaving
FULL NAME OF COMPANY

  Responsibilities: (less detailed)

  Results: (less detailed)

  Reason for leaving:

Date of starting to date of leaving
FULL NAME OF COMPANY

  Responsibilities: *(Note: If resume is in proper sequence, this and*
  Results: *ensuing employments will usually be of less*
  Reason for leaving: *importance and correspondingly less detailed)*

MISCELLANEOUS EMPLOYMENTS
Dates can be approximate, but should indicate time frame of period
involved (1965–1975)

  Group your minor (miscellaneous) employments stating in general
  type of work. If you are under 25, group your part-time employments, particularly during school years.

  Example:
  1970–1975 Self-employed. Mowed lawns.
  1976–1977 McDonalds Restaurant. Bus boy.

PREPARATION OF THE RESUME

JOB OBJECTIVE

The Job Objective is the "soul" of your resume and should be given first and foremost consideration. Job Objective says what you want to do and it should say it as clearly and concisely as possible.

Decide the type of a job for which you are best equipped by reason of your temperament, personal preferences, capabilities and experience—then state it. If it is in sales, what kind? Is management your goal? Any travel restrictions? This would then be stated "Position in tangible sales leading to management. Prefer limited travel." Note examples on the actual resumes in Part Two of this book. Unless you have strong geographical preferences, do not state them. It serves only to narrow the scope of your availability.

Suppose you do not have very definite or well-defined objectives; or perhaps you have several. You may consider comprehensive job counseling, or at least discuss your background with an employment counselor to determine the best statement of your objectives. In any event, we urge you to avoid the "all purpose—will do anything" type of objective. You cannot sell a product successfully unless you are specific about its advantages to the buyer.

EMPLOYMENT

List employment in reverse chronological order (your present or last job *first*, etc.) Be certain you list starting and leaving dates, your position title, exact name of company and present address. If the company had changed name or address since you were there, state "Jones-Smith Co., 114 Main St., Newark, N.J. (formerly known as Smith Co., 90 So. Ave., Camden, N.J.)." Company line is for purposes of identification only and is not necessary when it is well known nationally, or if identification is obvious from the company name. Example: "Morris *Lumber* Company."

If salary is to be stated at all, it should be stated in one line on the synopsis page. To state salary is to lose your bargaining power. Also, if you say that you are earning $15,000 while applying for an $18,000 job, you narrow your chances of getting the higher figure. Conversely, you may be unhappy in your $20,000 job and are willing to take less money in more agreeable work. Your present salary could scare off a prospective employer.

At the interview, your salary will, and *must*, be discussed. However, for resume purposes, showing the percentage of increase (if noteworthy) in the amplification portion is a safe middle road to travel. At the executive level, we suggest "salary in low, medium, or high five figures" as a method of establishing your level without pinpointing the exact amount. This can appear in one line of the synopsis page.

EDUCATION

The further you are away from school, the less educational detail is required. For other than the recent graduate, use the form shown on page 4 to set forth your education clearly and concisely—fitting it, of course, to your particular situation. Make certain that the name and location of schools are correct, as well as the dates attended, especially if your education shows a continued effort at self-improvement, as indicated by fairly recent courses.

A recent graduate has little but education for sale. Therefore, he should cover this area thoroughly, listing not only his majors and minors, but any and all subjects related to his field of interest. We also suggest listing semester hours and grades when better than average. Extracurricular activities are important for they indicate a well-rounded personality and demonstrate a social awareness. This importance, of course, diminishes with time—so again, the older you are, and the further away from school, the fewer items you should list.

Work during college for the recent graduate can be shown on the synopsis page under "Employment," and/or on page 5 (the Amplification part of your resume) as space permits.

Do *not* omit your education because it is limited. It will "out," so anticipate this by enlarging upon it where possible, by listing company courses, home-study courses, etc. This indicates a desire for self-education readily understood by the often sympathetic employer who (like you) may not have had the opportunity for extensive formal education. The same man will not be equally sympathetic to amateurish attempts at bluffing an education you do not have.

PERSONAL DATA

There is no pat response to the frequently asked question, "How much personal information shall I give in my resume?" It is illegal in many states to attach a photograph, and the law allows an employer to ask *only* the year you were born, *not* your age. However, there is no law that says you can't volunteer whatever personal information may give you an edge.

Personal information is your visual introduction and it is important. The employer is hiring you, the individual, as well as your set of qualifications, and one can balance (or even offset) the other. Consequently, it is common sense to list only flattering descriptive data. For example, if you're a sleek 5′5″ female or a trim 6′ male, give your height and weight; if not, skip it. In some positions, age (maturity) is a plus. On the other hand, if you're reluctant about revealing an exact figure, and you're over 35, say "mature." If you're under 35, volunteering your actual age and date of birth could be to your advantage in this youth-oriented society, so why not do so? In any event, do not ignore the age question completely. Employers have a way of reading the wrong information into omissions.

Marital status can get sticky, but don't let it. If you have been divorced and have no dependent children, you are "single." If you have been divorced and remarried, you are "married" with as many children as are currently dependent and under your roof.

Health is always "excellent" to "good" unless you have a specific handicap or problem that places some limitations on job performance. For example, a bad or injured leg would not interfere with the performance of an accountant. In this book, there appears a resume of a woman who is a "Diabetes Mellitus, Class I" and her health is listed as "Excellent." This type of diabetes requires only that her hours be regular, an important factor in diabetic management. Fact is merely mentioned, not dwelled upon.

Owning your home or apartment tends to say "roots," stability and order is in your life. Stating this could be a plus. Hobbies can flesh out your portrait as can club affiliations and other outside interests. We conjure up a different version of a person who plays tennis and loves the theatre from one who plays chess and loves to read. A word of warning, however: do not give yourself a fancied hobby. Employers have been known to select a listed hobby for detailed discussion, for the sole purpose of testing the credibility of the resume.

MILITARY SERVICE

If service is recent and extensive, it can be "headlined" on the synopsis page and amplified. Otherwise, a lone line regarding it, under "personal," will serve.

The recently discharged service man (like the recent graduate) has little but his service experience, education, and training to sell, and should give these emphasis. Generally speaking, select the functions you performed most capably and relate them to a civilian occupational field. This is a specialized type of resume and does not always lend itself to the resume "mold."

ANALYSIS OF AMPLIFICATION PREPARATION

Before we discuss writing up the details of your history, let us review briefly just what a resume is. A resume, in essence, is a piece of direct mail advertising—*and the product is YOU*.

Effective, direct mail advertising is: (1) attractive in appearance; (2) provocative in content; (3) positive in approach. Emphasis is *always* on what the product has done and is capable of doing, *never* on what it has not done and why. Keep this foremost in your mind when you are preparing your own "direct mail advertising."

As we have said previously, the sole purpose of a resume is to arouse interest and to get you an interview. Save some ammunition for that interview, but get enough into the resume to make the interviewer want to know more about you—to call you in and talk with you. Strive to sound like a good investment.

RESPONSIBILITIES

State in what capacity you were employed and what you were expected to do. Also state level of responsibility. Use phrases like "completely responsible for," etc. Many jobs involve familiarity with certain kinds of equipment or processes. For instance, in data processing: state any equipment within your experience, and what you are able to do with it—operate, wire, program; in purchasing: state type of materials, components, etc., you have purchased; in manufacturing: state kinds of equipment involved; in personnel: state what steps you took in the grievance procedure, unions dealt with, number of employees in plant.*

RESULTS

This is the body of your resume for here you set yourself apart from the "herd" through accomplishment. Everyone has responsibilities, but not everyone fulfills them to the same degree. Results give you stature above and beyond a formal (sometimes meaningless) title bestowed on you by a firm. Again, remember the advertising approach. Point up what you can do by showing what you have done. You must sell your value to a company as deftly and effectively as it sells its products to the public. For example, if you are a salesman, alert the employer to the fact that you are a good salesman by the simple expedient of showing increased sales volume. Perhaps you only maintained sales volume but you did so under unusual difficulties. State what they were, and how you overcame them.

In many fields, results cannot be measured in so simple a fashion. However, salary increase is a "result," promotion is a "result," increased responsibilities can be a "result." You might have received recognition in the form of an award or completed a project outside the framework of your responsibilities and received no particular recognition for it. Reward yourself in your resume by stating what you did. If necessary, list such extracurricular activity under a heading "Special Accomplishment."

If you have been with one firm a long time it is sometimes difficult to show concrete results. Employ the "progression" technique. The principle involved here is simple. To have started as a delivery boy and to have ended up as a file clerk, makes you a more important file clerk.

*If your most recent job represents your highest skills (as it probably does), we suggest that you give it most space. If it has resulted from a definite progression from earlier jobs, such jobs can be covered more briefly.

8

State what you did in general terms (selling, construction, general office work) but where possible state name of company. This gives credence to your statements. Also make certain you give the approximate dates this miscellaneous work period covered. The purpose of this grouping is twofold: (1) it shortens your resume and yet it still accounts for all your working years; (2) it avoids the impression of job-hopping.

REASON FOR LEAVING

Ordinarily the reason for leaving should be given for each employment to which you give an individual listing. Don't get involved or verbose. A simple "for better job" or "to improve status" will often do it.

On the other hand, at times the reason for leaving cannot be stated tersely because actually it came about through a complex situation involving other people, kind of work, rate of pay, and a variety of other factors. Try to tell your story clearly and concisely while avoiding such phrases as "no chance for advancement" (why did you take such a job?). "Arrived at dead-end" reflects more favorably upon you. "Disagreement with management" can be less peevishly stated as "Management policies not conducive to advancement in foreseeable future." "Salary did not keep pace with increased productivity" says more for you than "No salary increase."

Eventually, an employer will probably want to cover these matters thoroughly, but for resume purposes brevity without bitterness is the rule. If all else fails, use the entirely safe and acceptable reason for leaving "will be discussed at interview."

LENGTH OF RESUME

We do not deem it advisable to make arbitrary statements on resume length. Length will vary to the same degree individual records vary. However, we have found the average record can be handled satisfactorily in two to three pages (counting synopsis sheet as one).

Occasionally a complex or highly varied record requires a fourth page to tell the story properly and/or avoid an undesirable overcrowded appearance. If the employer likes what he sees at a glance, his appetite is whetted for detail; therefore, he proceeds with an eye to content rather than page number. For practical purposes, a good rule of thumb is two-page minimum, four-page maximum.

PERSON AND TENSE

Although the rule is not rigid, our surveys show the third person and the past tense (telegraphic style) are preferred. Consider these phrasings:

1) "As a result of my efficient discharge of duties, I was promoted."
2) "As a result of his efficient discharge of duties, he was promoted."
3) "As a result of efficient discharge of duties, was promoted."

We believe the latter two phrasings are more pleasing to read. Many self-prepared resumes make the mistake of being too modest. Deleting the first person "I" may make it easier for you to give yourself proper credit without feeling boastful.

REFERENCES

Unless references are requested, most employers are unimpressed by such a list. There are a number of reasons for this: (1) Any name you list is obviously a "friend," understandably prejudiced in your favor. (2) The word of a past employer is not necessarily significant. Prospective employers are aware that it is not an uncommon practice for a past employer to give a likable, yet unsatisfactory worker, a "break" in the form of a good reference. These and other factors serve to render the reference list of little or no value. For resume purposes, stating "References Available" is a safe, standard, and acceptable practice.

You may disagree with us in regard to our philosophy of stating specific references. If so, there is no harm in listing your references. We simply don't believe it does much good in the resume itself.

PHYSICAL PREPARATION OF RESUME

As you are not inclined to buy a product in a soiled wrapper, an employer does not "buy" you on cheap paper, messy with erasures and misspelled words. A resume *must* be typed. A well-typed resume is always acceptable (never a carbon). Your alternative is to have your resume duplicated by a professional business service (check Yellow Pages, usually under "Photocopy"). Type, or have typed, your initial copy following our format so it may be used by the business service as a guide in setting it up properly. You need not be concerned about spacing, placing, etc., for any reputable firm which specializes in this type of work can, and will, set it up attractively. The cost of duplication on good bond of 50 to 100 copies of a two- to three-page resume usually will not exceed 10¢ per page—and since your position may hinge upon it, it is money well-spent.

Resist all suggestions or advice to use a marker pen on your resume for "emphasis." Proper emphasis is achieved in a resume by clear format and concise, meaty content. Colored underscoring and marginal notes are childish.

Do not use a "resume cover." A few die-hards still persist in encasing their typed resume in expensive cardboard or vinyl covers. Don't be one of them. It's the mark of an amateur, show-off, or both. More importantly, however, covers irritate prospective employers. They don't fit in their letter files. They do fit in their round one.

Answering Classified Ads

"Wanted: mature, responsible, full-time sales lady"..."Young, attractive girl-Friday" ..."Appliance company seeking reliable young man for management trainee program." If you are very much your own person, you are entirely within your legal rights to respond to any of these classified advertisements regardless of your sex. Each of these ads is a violation of the 1964 Civil Rights Act, which specifically prohibits discrimination on the basis of sex in all aspects of employment including help-wanted advertising. If you would rather not do battle, but as a concerned citizen would like to see this law enforced, you can do so by reporting such discriminatory recruiting practices to the Equal Employment Opportunity Commission, 1800 G Street, N.W., Washington, D.C. 20506.

Before answering any ad anywhere it is assumed that you have armed yourself with a good resume. The final step is the covering letter for your resume. Specific ad answering technique does not vary appreciably from any good covering letter of application except for one point: follow the advertisement line so as to sound tailor-made for the job. For example, if you are replying to the ad for the mature saleswoman, you should slant as follows:

Dear Sir:

In response to your advertisement in the November 5th issue of the Herald Tribune, I am over forty, in good health, own my own home and car, and am presently in a position to accept a full-time job.

If the position you offer should involve evening over-time or occasional inventory week-end, in that my family is grown and my responsibilities discharged, I should be able and willing to take on responsibilities for you.

I shall look forward to discussing the sales position with you personally. My phone number and other pertinent details may be found in my attached resume.

Cordially,

GENERAL COVERING LETTER

Always enclose a covering letter when you mail out a resume.

Cover letters should be individually typed and signed. Anything else indicates a serious lack of any real interest, and a lack of elementary business courtesy as well.

Your covering letter should be brief and follow the general guidelines given below.

1. Address your letter to a specific person. Employers are people, and people tend to be complimented when you know their name and title. Consequently, it's worthwhile to make an effort to find it out.

If the company you are applying to is located nearby, phone and ask whoever answers for the name of the President, Sales Manager, Personnel Manager, whatever. It's not necessary to identify yourself or your reason for calling. If you should be pressed, a disarming "I want to write him (her) a letter" will usually do the trick.

If the job is important enough, this call should be made wherever the company is located. Don't rely on some friend's recollection of a name or personnel records. They get out of date rapidly, and a letter addressed to a predecessor immediately labels you as a person with a certain carelessness for meaningful detail.

2. Your letter need not cover the same ground as your resume. It should merely sum up what you have to offer and act as an introduction for your resume.

3. Let your letter reflect your individuality, but avoid appearing familiar, overbearing, humorous, or cute.

4. With local firms, take the initiative in suggesting that you telephone for an interview.

5. With out-of-town or state firms, it is imperative that you indicate willingness to make the trip for a personal interview. Better yet, give dates when you could be in the area for an interview.

SAMPLE COVERING LETTER

1877 Orange Ave. Sarasota, FL 33579

Mr. George Howe, Manager
Howe Realtors
29 Prospect St.
Sarasota, Florida 33581

Dear Mr. Howe:

I want to be a real estate sales person with the Howe corporation.

With my recently acquired Florida Real Estate License, I know that working for your highly respected company would be the ideal way for me to learn the practical sales skills needed to supplement enthusiasm and education.

At present, I realize that my most useful skills may be typing and knowledge of general office procedures. However, I have no inflated aspirations of starting at the top. I expect to reach it, but first I am anxious to learn and for an opportunity to demonstrate my ability.

May I call your secretary for an interview appointment?
Thank you.

Sincerely,

(Signed: Lois Gunther)

Lois Gunther

enc: resume

(A generally good approach when sending out a resume "cold," i.e., without any knowledge that an opening may exist. Requires a bit more "self-sell" to generate interest in getting resume read.)

RESUME FOR COVERING LETTER

Resume of:
Lois Gunther

1877 Orange Ave.
Sarasota, FL 33579
Phone: (803) 922–0778

JOB OBJECTIVE

Real Estate Sales Person

EDUCATION

1980	Principles and Practice of Real Estate St. Loo's College (extension)
Other:	Real Estate License Law Course Reagon Specialized School of Instruction
License:	Florida Real Estate Salesman's License Received November, 1979 Notary-Public-at-large, State of Florida Commission valid through 1982
College:	University of Florida B.S. in History

EXPERIENCE

10/79-Pres.	Boomhower Real Estate Company Arcadia, FL
10/78–10/79	Lindsey Title and Mortgage Miami, FL
1976–1978	Lee County Schools, Ft. Myers, FL History teacher
Other:	General office work, sales

PERSONAL

Born:	1954 in Phoenix, Arizona. Divorced; one child.
Appearance:	Height 5'8"; wt. 120; Health: excellent.
Finances:	Own car, home, income property.
Hobbies:	Sports car rallying; sewing; reading.
Affiliations:	Sarasota Board of Realtors Florida Board of Realtors National Board of Realtors

(FOR AMPLIFICATION PLEASE SEE FOLLOWING)

EMPLOYMENT HIGHLIGHTS

October 1979-Present
BOOMHOWER REALTORS

Accepted position as sales person with assurance that would enter planned sales training program under guidance of an experienced member of the sales force.

Program failed to materialize; would make change to company that would provide background training in the practical aspects of selling to complement and embellish theories and principles learned in acquiring recent real estate license.

10/78–10/79
LINDSEY TITLE AND MORTGAGE

Accepted position as mortgage clerk to obtain practical experience in real estate field. Responsible for shipping out recorded closing instruments and typing of title insurance policies.

Was given occasional opportunities to go into field for sales indoctrination and found this to be best area and ultimate goal.

Reason for leaving: To accept offer of sales training leading to full-time sales position with major firm above.

1976–1978
LEE COUNTY SCHOOLS

Taught History at Junior High Level; also responsible for school library.

During summer of 1977, was offered position as manager of the Taylor Galleries in Ft. Myers. Encompassed myriad responsibilities including sales promotion of rare paintings, sculpture and sundry objects d'art. Customers ranged from general tourists to visiting dignitaries.

Handled all books, all relevant correspondence; closed sales. Offered position following summer; was unable to accept.

GENERAL

Well-rounded background with emphasis on meeting, dealing with, and selling to the public.

REFERENCES

In confidence, on request.

(Note: Ms. Gunther is changing fields; consequently her former profession is de-emphasized in favor of her newly acquired education in her present field, plus a focus on the sales aspects of her former record—a needed tool in the new field.)

Helpful Hints For The Interview

The purpose of the interview is to evaluate your

1. **Personality**
2. **Background and qualifications for the job sought**

The following are suggestions for you to observe in order to do your best in each of the foregoing areas in which you will be appraised during the interview.

BASICS

Appearance:
Be neat and well groomed, and dress appropriately. An interview is neither the time nor place to do your own thing or be your own person. Dress to fit the occasion. If you are applying for a white collar job, pants suits are now considered acceptable for women; however, unless you are applying for a highway flag-person's job, skip the jeans. Long hair and beards on men have also found acceptance (when combed and clean).

Courtesy:
Old fashioned courtesy can be expected to pay dividends. Begin in the anteroom. Astute employers have been known to check with trusted employees as to their impressions of an applicant before, as well as after, being interviewed. Making a pass at an attractive receptionist is not necessarily effective (if she's the boss's girl it can be fatal); however, genuine courtesy is rare and remembered. During the interview you can't go too far wrong by saying yes-sir and no-sir to your prospective employer, asking permission to smoke (if you see an ashtray and do), and thanking him for his time when the interview is concluded.

Poise:
Show confidence, but not arrogance. Don't act overly humble or hang-dog by playing up your limitations. You may feel ill at ease (employers understand this), but don't spotlight your nervousness with annoying outward manifestations (fiddling with your hair or glasses, brushing imaginary things off your clothes). Your body language will be talking louder than you are.

Frankness and Honesty:
Be direct. If you don't know the answer, say no. Describe your experience, skills, and abilities precisely and accurately. "Oh what a tangled web we weave, when first we practice to deceive" was written by Sir Walter Scott—but it could have been written by any prevaricating job hunter.

Vitality:
Act alive, alert, and enthusiastic, but beware of a falsely effervescent, gushing, put-on personality. It's called "phoney" and it's number one on the prospective employer's "Most Unwanted List."

Knowledge:
Do your homework. Report for the interview with a clear knowledge of the company's operations. Know what they do, make, or sell so that you will be in a position to show how you will fit into the operation, and why it will be to the company's advantage that you do so. Skilled interviewers can quickly detect familiarity with their operation and they are flattered as well as favorably impressed.

15

The following strategy has been developed from the experiences of employers all over the country who have conducted countless interviews.

1. Let the interviewer lead with the questioning. Answer only what is asked (no more, no less); then wait for the next question. Don't try to fill in all the "silence." Studying your reaction to a conversational pause is sometimes an interview test. Babble and you flunk.

2. Pay strict attention so that you will fully understand the question. If you do not, politely request a repeat or a re-phrasing.

3. Don't interrupt. Sometimes an employer will state a hypothetical situation, then ask the question. Give him time to finish and give yourself time to think before you reply. Interviews are not conducted with a stop watch, and a hasty, ill-considered answer can be disastrous.

4. Don't strive to give the answer you *think* the employer wants. Experienced interviewers quickly recognize this game. Strive for honesty and consistency. If you think you are right on a point, stick with it; if you are wrong on a point, admit it.

5. Don't be a comedian. The employer considers hiring you as a serious business and you'll help your cause by adopting a similar approach. Pleasantries and pleasantness are always in order; smart talk and small talk—never.

6. Unless you are pressed for detail, don't spend too much time talking about your present or past employments. And never— ever—knock you present or past employer. "Personality conflict" will say it all for the initial interview (and perhaps forever). You will have gained two things: (1) you haven't permanently closed a door that life may steer you through again, and (2) you

establish yourself as a person of honor and restraint.

7. Don't overplay your technical knowledge. Your resume (the good one that got you your interview) tells what you know. At this point the employer wants to know what you are.

8. During the initial interview, don't spend too much time asking about the chances for advancement or subsequent salary scales. Give the impression that you are confident that, once given the opportunity to prove yourself, the future will take care of itself. Employers are not in the business of hiring persons they expect to stand still.

9. If you are over 50, get mentally set for the fact there is no way you are going to hide it. Hopefully your resume has reflected your honest age, and the fact you are there indicates that the employer is interested in your experience.

   Keeping in mind that no younger competitor can match your experience is often an important confidence factor. At all costs avoid arrogance because of your background, and the tendency to be patronizing to the "young squirt" interviewing you. You are there because you need work, and your age will not seriously mitigate against you unless it is obvious that you have contempt for the young, and/or are too set in your ways and thinking to accept new ways of doing things.

10. If it becomes obvious that you are not the right person for the job, at the conclusion of the interview ask the interviewer (if the organization is large) if there is another area in which you might be qualified. If the organization is small, ask him if he might suggest a place or company who could logically use your services. He often can, and if you've made a good impression he often will.

COMMONLY ASKED INTERVIEW QUESTIONS AND
HOW TO ANSWER THEM

1. *Tell me something about yourself.*

   Know your resume details and state them concisely.

2. *Why do you want to work for us?*

   Do whatever research possible ahead of time to be ready for this question. Explain that you are impressed with their policies, reputation, working conditions, physical plant—whatever seems germane.

3. *Why should I hire you?*

   Because you are uniquely qualified and your personal goals coincide with theirs. Explain what you can bring to the job.

4. *Why did you leave your last job?*

   Tell it like your resume says.

5. *Why are you thinking of leaving your present job?*

   Be honest, be brief, but be prepared. Internal politics, dead-end, too much pressure, too little salary are all acceptable, understandable reasons.

6. *What are your strengths?*

   Careful study of your resume in advance will prepare you for this question, plus help you document your reply. Does it reveal leadership? Ambition? Loyalty? Determination? Ability to work under pressure? To cope? To get along with people? Steady work record? Extraordinary abilities (sales, administrative)?

7. *What are your weaknesses?*

   Nobody's perfect, but be easy on yourself. Don't relate anything directly to your performance on the job. You can turn this to your advantage by thinking it through ahead of time. For example. "I have a temper—but one of my strengths is that I have learned to control it."

8. *Where do you expect to be ten or twenty years from now?*

   This is a favorite. Think it through carefully and resist all temptations to make a flip response. "In your job" can be a dangerous reply to an insecure man or woman. Expecting promotions and salary increases commensurate with your good work is good. If you have an opportunity to study the chain of command and know exactly whereof you speak, being specific is better.

9. *What is the minimum salary you would find acceptable?*

   Know the salary range of the job and inquire if this is in line with their scale. Stress job satisfaction and willingness to accept a starting figure you can genuinely live with. Negotiate if necessary stressing your qualifications.

10. *When could you start work here?*

    If not working—immediately! If working, play fair with your present employer—a week to two weeks notice if in a non-supervisory capacity; one month minimum in management or supervisory capacity.

QUESTIONS YOU SHOULD ASK A PROSPECTIVE EMPLOYER

1. What would my duties and responsibilities be? Or, if it is a large firm, they may have a prepared job description. Ask for it.

2. If salary has not yet been discussed, broach it in the same manner discussed under interviewer questions.

3. For whom will I be working for and with? What will my hours be?

4. What are my opportunities for advancement? Raises?

5. What are my opportunities for additional training and/or education?

6. What are your employee benefits?

7. What are your (company/firm/store) policies on: holidays, lunch, dress, smoking, coffee breaks?

8. Are employees paid every week—every two weeks?

9. Is there any additional information with which I can provide you to aid your evaluation of me for this position?

10. May I ask when I can expect a decision regarding this position?

SOCIAL SECURITY

SOCIAL SECURITY CARDS

A social security number can be issued at any age if it is needed, but you *must* have a number if your work is covered by the social security law. Show your card to your employer when you start work or when you change jobs so that your wages will be properly credited to your social security earnings record at the headquarters of the Social Security Administration in Baltimore, Maryland.

You must have a social security number to get credit for your earnings. When you change jobs, don't give your new employer your number from memory—always *show* him your card. If you give him a wrong number, your earnings may not get entered on your record. The same goes for your name. If you change your name (for example, if you get married—or divorced and resume your maiden name), be sure to get a new card with your current name—but with your *old number*. If you lose your social security card, the following form illustrates procedure for getting a replacment. The social security office emphasizes you should have but *one social security number in your lifetime*. If you ever need a duplicate, be certain you state you already have a number (even though you may not know what it is). By listing your correct name and birthdate, it can be tracked down.

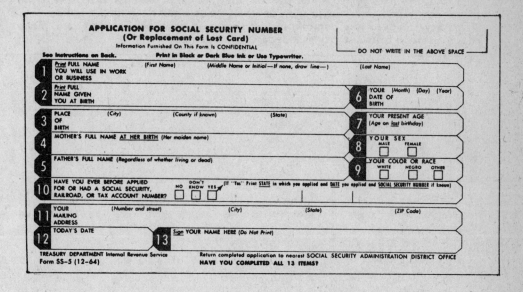

YOUR EARNINGS RECORD

Your employer is required to give you a form showing the amount of your earnings that count for social security. He does this at the end of the year (or when you stop working for him if it is before the end of the year). These receipts (usually a W-2 form "Wage and Tax Statement") will help you should there be an error in the amount of earnings reported on the social security record.

The social security administration has a special lifetime earnings record for you at its headquarters in Baltimore, Maryland. Year after year, for as long as your work is covered by social security, reports on your earnings are sent to them and the amounts added to your record by computer. This record is available to you at any time, and will be sent at no charge merely by filling out the card shown below (available at your social security office for the asking).

It is prudent to request this every three years or so, to make certain the social security taxes you are paying are being properly credited to your social security account. If there is an error, the more recently it was made the easier it is to correct. In some instances, after approximately three years have passed an error cannot be corrected; the record stands.

REQUEST FOR STATEMENT OF EARNINGS

SOCIAL SECURITY NUMBER →

DATE OF BIRTH →   MONTH   DAY   YEAR

Please send a statement of my Social Security earnings to:

NAME { MISS MRS. MR. } _____

STREET & NUMBER _____

CITY & STATE _____ ZIP CODE _____

Print Name and Address In Ink Or Use Typewriter

SIGN YOUR NAME HERE (DO NOT PRINT) _____

Sign your own name only. Under the law, information in your social security record is confidential and anyone who signs another person's name can be prosecuted.

If you have changed your name from that shown on your social security card, please copy your name below exactly as it appears on your card.

2

Sample Resumes

The sample resumes in this part of the book cover practically every area of job application. They were prepared by a professional resume writing organization whose sole function is the preparation of resumes. Consequently, it is essential that they keep in constant touch with employers nationwide to determine their preferences in the content and construction of resumes.

The resumes presented here are excellent models for you to follow since they embody many years of practical, professional experience and research in successful resume preparation.

An added feature of the resumes that follow is the explanatory note (in italics) at the bottom of each resume. These analyses should prove most helpful in guiding you in your use of these model resumes.

Key to Sample Resumes According to Occupational Area

We suggest the following procedure for quickly locating the model resumes that you should use as a pattern for writing your own: Find the general area in which you are interested in the groups on the following page. If you cannot find the exact position for which you are applying, look for the job titles that are closest to your desired job.

Read *all* of the resumes in your chosen group; this will help you to direct your resume specifically to the field in which you are interested. You will be able to pick up valuable ideas from each of these resumes—ideas that may be neatly incorporated into your own personal resume.

However, don't confine yourself to the resumes in just one group. Thumb through the entire resume section, paying special attention to the editor's comments at the bottom of some pages—these can show you how various problems are treated in professionally written resumes, and will provide valuable hints for writing your own. In this way you will be likely to compose a most effective job-getting resume— a resume which may turn out to be a vital factor in your landing the job you really want.

Synopsis of Resume of: 418 Delancey Place
JOSEPH MORGAN   Omaha, NB 61855
Certified Public Accountant   Phone: (402) 739–2331

JOB OBJECTIVE

Treasurer or Controller with medium-sized company.

EMPLOYMENT

1974–Present	TREASURER & DIRECTOR (both of company & subsidiary) Henry Morris Co., Omaha, NB Lincoln Machinery Co., Lincoln, NB
1966–1974	VICE PRES., CONTROLLER, SECRETARY Bloomington Perforating Co., St. Paul, MN
1963–1966	SR. ACCOUNTANT in Public Accounting firm. Charge of audits and tax work. Richard Moriarty & Co., C.P.A., Chicago, IL
1960–1963	PUBLIC ACCOUNTING James Platt, C.P.A., Chicago, IL
1958–1960	Period while attending college (nights) and prior to service: Southern Nat. bank-teller.

EDUCATION

1958–1962
(evenings)
	University of Chicago
	  Degree: B.S.
	  Major: Accounting; "A" average

1953–1957	Florida Technical Institute, Jacksonville, FL One year full time; balance evenings.

PERSONAL

Born:	3/2/35 in Jacksonville, FL Height 6'; wt. 190 lbs.
Married:	Wife graduate of U. of Chicago; no children.
Health:	Good; no physical limitations.
Residence:	Rents home; free to relocate.
Affiliations:	Midwest Chapt. C.P.A.; National Inst. C.P.A.
Service:	U.S. Navy Seaman Recruit to Lt. (jg). Honorably released; no reserve obligation.

(FOR AMPLIFICATION PLEASE SEE FOLLOWING)

Normally company dollar volume can be used as indicator of level of accounting responsibilities. In this instance company volume was so small it was omitted in favor of number of employees.

Amplified Resume   Joseph Morgan

EMPLOYMENT HIGHLIGHTS

1974–Present
HENRY MORRIS CO. (200 employees)
Multi-plant manufacturer of corrugated or fibre box machinery

As Treasurer and Director of the company and subsidiary, (Lincoln Machinery Co.), has control of all accounting, company financing, and all employees in these fields.

Results:
By system changes has improved and speeded informative and permanent records, while reducing clerical and administrative salaries by $70,000 per annum. Assisted in increasing profits; company financial strength had increased substantially.

Reason for change:
Desires post with larger company offering remuneration commensurate with responsibilities.

1966–1974
BLOOMINGTON PERFORATING CO.
Perforated metal - 75 employees

Originally employed as Controller. Promoted to Vice President, Controller and Secretary. Had full charge of all accounting operations and personnel. Consulted on financial aspects of business.

Results:
Company experienced period of successful operation and growth. Has letters from superiors attesting to fact his activities contributed in large measure.

Reason for change:
To accept better position with larger company.

REFERENCES

Available

Synopsis of Resume of:
LOUIS GLEESON

35 Fountain St.
Elgin, IL 60102
Phone: (312) 793–5357

OBJECTIVE

Position in Accounting utilizing supervisory experience. Potential with long-term benefits.

EXPERIENCE

1980 - Present   BROOKSIDE CLUB & RESTAURANT, Elgin, Ill.
Night Auditor.

1960–1979   GARDEN PHOTO ENGRAVING CO., INC., Mineola, N.Y.
Business Manager - Corporate Director.
Company liquidated. Relocated in Illinois.

EDUCATION

Hofstra University, Hempstead, N.Y.
Major: Business/Bookkeeping/Accounting.

Skills: Burroughs L5000 computer system and P/R & A/R;
NCR Bookkeeping Machine; typewriter (40 wpm).

PERSONAL

Born: 1934; single; height 6'2"; wt. 170 lbs.; health - excellent.
Finances: Good order. Owns car, rents apt., free to relocate.
Hobbies: Ice skating; fishing; spectator sports.
Affiliations: Administrative Management Society.

(FOR AMPLIFICATION SEE FOLLOWING)

Divorced "displaced" man by virtue of long term employment termination and decision to move to new area and start anew. Is overqualified for present position; consequently given short shrift.

Amplified Resume   Louis Gleeson

EMPLOYMENT HIGHLIGHTS

January 1980–Present

Accepted interim position as night auditor for large, prestigious club. Responsible for auditing all customer tickets for food and beverage daily. Reads out the cash registers and balances sales for the day to register read-out. Writes up daily report of all business transacted for that day.

Reason for desiring change:
Eager for better paying position with long-term benefits more in line with heavy experience in accounting and supervision.

1960–1979
GARDEN PHOTO ENGRAVING CO. INC.

Accepted position as Administrative Assistant following honorable discharge from the Air Force.

Promoted to General Business Manager responsible for all finances of the corporation: banking, accounts receivable and payable, payroll, taxes, as well as for government classified material.

Bonded, with SECRET Security Clearance, dictated correspondence, supervised book-keeper, credit manager and clerks. Kept detailed records of sales; balanced all books monthly. Instituted, operated and taught operation of Burroughs L5000 computer system and P/R & A/R.

Steady raise in salary from initial $5,000 to high five figures.

Reason for leaving:
Company liquidated. Made decision to relocate to Illinois and establish permanent residence.

REFERENCES

Please no contact with present employer until after interview.

Synopsis of Resume of:
DAVID L. MC GRAW, Jr.

47 Beecher Place
Bangor, ME 04401
Phone: (207) 822–9177

JOB OBJECTIVE

Position as artist, designer, creative writer for advertising or promotion work.
Industrial advertising or agency.

EMPLOYMENT

1978–12/79	MECHANICAL PASTE-UP IN DESIGN - Art Department Langie Paper Container Corp., Bangor, ME
1976–1978	ADVERTISING MANAGER Jewett Dept. Store, 29 Third St., Bangor, ME
1973–1976	FREELANCE - Augusta, Maine area.
1970–1973	CHIEF OF JEWELRY DESIGN Best Arts Inc., 900 Tremont Blvd., Bangor, ME
1967–1970	POSTER DESIGNER & RUBBER PLATE ENGRAVER Porter Wells Inc., 308 Prince St., Boston, MA

Prior	Salem, Massachusetts:
	    Becks Dept. Store - Assistant window trimmer.
	    Makin Adv. Agency - Layout, design, copy writing.
	    Freer Photographers - Home photography.
	(Left each position voluntarily to improve status).

EDUCATION

1960–1965	Maryland Institute College of Art, Baltimore, MD Left voluntarily for financial reasons. Courses included: Advertising Design, Photography Interior Decorating, Illustration, Life Drawing.

PERSONAL

Born:	2/17/42 in Salem, MA. Height 5'10"; weight 176 lbs.
Married	Wife graduate of Hood College; no children.
Health:	Excellent.
Hobbies:	Painting; camping; fishing.
Affiliations:	Bd. member Bangor Memorial Art Gallery.

(FOR AMPLIFICATION PLEASE SEE FOLLOWING)
Field in which pictures and samples are literally more significant than a thousand resume words.
Therefore resume merely points up training and experience indicating, wherever possible, samples of work
available for review. To enclose or attach such samples could restrict opportunity to be invited for
interview.

Amplified Resume   David L. McGraw, Jr.

EMPLOYMENT HIGHLIGHTS

1978–12/79
LANGIE PAPER CONTAINER CORP.
Mfrs.: cartons, packing containers

Employed in Art Department to perform mechanical paste-up of designs to be applied to packages, boxes, or cartons, primarily of food container type. In addition, assisted in actual design of packages.
Reason for leaving: Business went bankrupt.

1976–1978
JEWETT DEPT. STORE

Employed as Advertising Manager. Prepared copy and art work. Did layouts for news media selecting material of reader interest, and slanting such material to acceptable style and store policy. Created and arranged store and window displays. Photographs of such displays, and samples of newspaper display ads are available for inspection.
Reason for leaving: To accept position above which appeared to offer greater potential.

1973–1976
FREELANCE

Assisted established designers; obtained commissions on own (restaurant murals, portraits, etc.) Wrote several articles on fishing and outdoor life (complete with photographs); had seven accepted for national publication; available for review.

1970–1973
BEST ARTS INC. (School pins, jewelry, etc.)

Employed as head of jewelry design. Worked from written description or rough sketch of desired article. Made and submitted accurate formal drawing of item to school or organization for approval. Upon acceptance, metal-die department used drawing for duplication. Samples of work available.

Reason for leaving: Resigned to do freelance work.

1967–1970
PORTER WELLS INC.

Employed as trainee in rubber plate engraving for reproduction of posters. Made pencil drawings on tracing paper which was rubbed down onto rubber plate and became guide to follow for hand cutting with engraving tools. Progressed into original creative poster design. Resigned to gain additional experience in other art fields.

References on Request

Synopsis of Resume of:
ELLIOT N. HALE

159 Antlers Dr.
Duluth, MN 55802
Phone: (218) 643−4962

POSITION OBJECTIVE

Patent Attorney

EXPERIENCE

1976–Present	PATENT ATTORNEY, (Associate) Armstron & McKenzie, Patent Attorneys Duluth, MN
1973–1976	PATENT ATTORNEY Bigelow Mfg. Co., Div. Gen. Bronze Corp. Pittsburgh, PA
1972–1973	PATENT ENGINEER General Electric Co., Wash. DC office.
1966–1972	Private Law Practice Philadelphia, PA
1965–1966	Field representative, Workmen's Compensation Board, Philadelphia, PA (1 yr. position concurrent with private practice)

QUALIFICATIONS

Education:	L.L.B. 1964 from Georgetown University, Wash. DC Admitted to Bar, State of Penna. 1965.
Certification:	Member Minnesota State Bar. Admission to practice before U.S. Patent Office, U.S. Court of Customs & Patent Appeals, U.S. Court of Claims, U.S. Supreme Court.

PERSONAL

Born:	5/26/38 in Harrisburg, PA. Height 6'2"; wt. 205 lbs.
Married:	Wife R.N.; 3 children, ages: 8, 6, and pre-school.
Health:	Good; no physical limitations.
Residence:	Rents home; free to relocate.
Hobbies:	Chess; golf; spectator sports.

(FOR AMPLIFICATION PLEASE SEE FOLLOWING)

This was originally a highly detailed resume, yet it bore poor results. The new resume (shown here) stresses certification and experience highlights to whet employer reading interest. Better than average speaking ability of applicant will sustain employer interest in detail during interview.

Amplified Resume

Elliot N. Hale

EXPERIENCE

1976–Present
ARMSTRON & MC KENZIE
Patent Attorneys

Association with firm to prepare and prosecute patent applications, advise and render opinions on infringement questions and related matters.

Content with association; however, feels income not in line with responsibilities. Desires industrial connection, preferably in New England area.

.1973–1976
BIGELOW MFG. CO., Div. Gen. Bronze Corp.

As patent attorney prepared and prosecuted patent applications covering the electrical and electro-mechanical arts.

Desired position which required not only preparation and prosecution of patent application, but infringement, licensing and litigations. Offered and accepted present post which promised added scope.

1972–1973
GENERAL ELECTRIC CO.

After discussion with head of G.E. Patent Division, was offered and accepted position as Patent Engineer in Wash. DC office. Made arrangements to study patent law; was admitted to practice before the U.S. patent office.

Family situation necessitated return to Pennsylvania area.

1966–1972
PRIVATE PRACTICE

Upon admission to the bar in 1965, set up office with partner in Philadelphia. Engaged in private practice of law which included the following: commercial practice, contract matters, real estate, receiverships and bankruptcy. Also engaged in the formation of, as well as serving as an officer for, various corporations. In addition, was clerk of Mortgage and Real Estate Committee for the Assembly in the Pennsylvania State Legislature.

Established excellent reputation; dissolved highly successful partnership to accept offer above which offered opportunity to pursue his interest in patent law.

REFERENCES

Available

Synopsis of Resume of:
LEONARD SORZANO

47 Eaton St.
Buffalo, NY 14206
Phone: (716) 650–7764

JOB OBJECTIVE

Supervisory position in carpentry. Residential preferred.

EMPLOYMENT

10/76–Present	FRANK BALLARD, General Contractor, Buffalo, NY Working carpenter foreman. (Yearly income has increased by $4,420 since start of employment).
1974–1976 and 1968–1971	SELF-EMPLOYED 1. Contractor, Carpenter - Syracuse, NY area. 2. Subcontractor - Tampa, Florida area.
1971–1974	ELECTRONICS DIV. OF GE., Syracuse, NY Group leader, jig and fixture maker. Resigned for outside work.
Prior	Miscellaneous short-term employments as carpenter's helper, mason, farm worker, during school vacation periods and prior service.

EDUCATION

Elwood Sr. High School, Clearwater, FL
   Graduated 1965.
North High (night) School, Syracuse, NY
   Courses in: Time Study, Sheet Metal Welding
   & Cutting, Blue Print Reading, Industrial
   Methods and Planning
Current: I.C.S. course in Architectual Drafting & Designing
   Continuous self study in construction procedures.

PERSONAL

Born:	10/7/47 in Clearwater, FL. Single. Height 5'11½"; weight 186 lbs.
Health:	Good; no physical limitations.
Residence:	Rents; free to relocate.

(FOR AMPLIFICATION PLEASE SEE FOLLOWING)
Record of competent workman organized so as to give at a glance clear comprehension of geographic and employment field moves, followed by logical explanation.

Amplified Resume   Leonard Sorzano

EMPLOYMENT

10/76–Present
FRANK BALLARD, General Contractor

Employed to take over the building or repair of homes contracted by Frank Ballard. On new work is given points of project, selects his carpenters, lays out the entire operation from cellar to the completed home ready for occupancy. Supervises all subcontracting (electrical, plumbing, etc.).

In remodeling, also takes over completely. Is given an idea of what is required, plans and completes work, often working without prints. Where bank loans are required by owners, frequently makes drawings of proposed work to be submitted to lending institutions. Works to budgets; knows how to keep within given amounts. Accustomed to directing personnel; able to get maximum effort from workers under his supervision.

Reason for desiring change: Work is not continuous; wishes connection with more active contractor.

SELF EMPLOYED

1968–1971
Became a subcontractor of carpenter work in Tampa, Florida. Employed crew of 8, and was employed by over 25 general contractors in various housing developments. Work included all types of carpentry from rough framing to cabinet work.

Estimates were profitable; every contract completed in specified time; earned excellent income. Family emergency necessitated return to north. Took position with General Electric (1971–1974); was in line for Industrial Engineering, when on physician's advice resigned for outdoor work to offset weakened condition brought on by pneumonia.

1974–1976
Employed up to 3 men; contracted work on residences, barns, etc. (new, repair, remodeling). Made reasonably good income; terminated operations on decision to accept excellent offer made by present employer.

GENERAL

Can lay out and cut rafters of all types. Familiar with use of transit in laying out buildings. Can lay out a home from cellar to finish. Can estimate time and material needed for carpenter and mason work. Draw prints. Has working knowledge of: mason, electrical and plumbing work.

REFERENCES

Available

Synopsis of Resume of:
SALLY POST

411 Gladsone St.
Miami, FL 33135
Phone: (305) 421–7594

JOB OBJECTIVE

Cashier

EMPLOYMENT

1978–Present   Cashier
Starlight Restaurant
1090 Madison St., Chicago, IL

1975–1978   Cashier
Avalon Theater
198 Michigan Blvd., Chicago, IL

1973–1974   Sales Clerk
The Fair (Department Store)
Chicago, IL

EDUCATION

High School: Jackson High School, Chicago, IL
Graduated 1973.

Other: Sales training course given by store in
Chicago, IL, included cash register
instruction.

PERSONAL

Born: 9/6/55 in Milwaukee, WI. Single. Height 5'8"; wt. 130 lbs.
Health: Good.
Hobbies: Swimming, bowling; social activities.

(FOR AMPLIFICATION PLEASE SEE FOLLOWING)
Showing good, steady work record (all in same locality), while putting equal emphasis on seriousness of intent to relocate permanently in entirely different area. At this level, first person tense acceptable and client more comfortable with the informality.

Amplified Resume   Sally Post

EMPLOYMENT HIGHLIGHTS

1978–Present
STARLIGHT RESTAURANT

Have heavy financial responsibility: act as cashier, make bank deposits, distribute payroll envelopes weekly. As this is a quality establishment catering to highest-type clientele, courtesy, tact, and conservative, tasteful dress is an essential part of position.

Reason for desiring change: Was given leave of absence several months ago to establish residence in Florida for a divorce. I found that Florida climate agrees with me since I have a slight sinus condition, and I should like to locate there permanently.

1975–1978
AVALON THEATER

Employed as ticket cashier on temporary basis; was offered and accepted job on full time basis after two week trial period.

Reason for leaving: Theater was sold for conversion to a supermarket.

1973–1974
THE FAIR (Dept. store)

Employed as sales clerk part-time during high school; offered and accepted full time employment following high school graduation.

Reason for leaving: Long hours and low pay.

GENERAL

Though I have lived in Chicago the greater part of my life, I no longer have any ties there, and find the Florida climate and way of life much more to my liking. I fully intend this to be a permanent move, and offer five solid years of working experience, plus determination to prove my worth in a position in the Florida area.

REFERENCES

Available

Synopsis of Resume of:
STEWART T. MORRIS

62 Crestview Pk.
Rogers City, MI 49779
Phone: (517) 813–8903

JOB OBJECTIVE

1. INDUSTRY: Personnel field, Sales, Public Relations. 2. SCHOOL: Guidance, Educational Administration.

EMPLOYMENT

1978–Present   SUPERINTENDENT OF SCHOOLS
Rogers City, MI

1969–1978   SUPERVISING PRINCIPAL
Board of Education, Cheboygan, MI

1959–1969   DIRECTOR PHYSICAL EDUCATION
Board of Education, Gaylord, MI

1958–1959   Teacher in one-room school (all attendant problems)
Fairview, MI

EDUCATION

1954–1958   State University of Michigan, Ann Arbor, MI
(Completed 5 year course in 4 years)
Degrees: B.S. in Physical Education.
        A.B. (cum laude) - Science Minor.
        M.S. in Education (1967)
Activities: Varsity basketball; all intramural sports;
        received cup for all-around athletic achievement;
        social fraternity - president Sr. yr.
Note: Total of 20 hours beyond Master's Degree,
        acquired as time and location have permitted.
        Expects to continue on same basis.

PERSONAL

Born: 6/5/35 in Toledo, OH. Height 5'11"; wt. 175 lbs.
Married: Wife graduate Stephens College for Women; 2 teenage children.
Health: Excellent; no physical limitations; last physical, 1980.
Residence: Owns home and summer cottage; willing to relocate.
Hobbies: Sports (active and spectator); Music Appreciation.
Affiliations: Rotary International; Michigan State Teachers Association;
Michigan State City and Village Superintendents; active in
local affairs - see following for complete listing.

(FOR AMPLIFICATION PLEASE SEE FOLLOWING)
Stressing success in handling people, as well as esteem in which applicant is held as indicated by elective office and membership in responsible organizations.

Amplified Resume   Stewart T. Morris

EMPLOYMENT HIGHLIGHTS

1978–Present
SUPERINTENDENT OF SCHOOLS
Employed as Superintendent of system composed of a Senior High, Junior High and four elementary schools.

Under his direction system has been centralized with outlying districts brought into it. Bus routes have been put into operation; approximately $9,000,000 in new buildings have been added (three complete buildings plus other additions); four bond issues have been proposed to and passed by the community.

Faculty has grown from 85 to 120; student body has increased from 1,500 to 2,700. Scholarship has been maintained at a high level. Pupil achievement averages are in top percentile of country; scholarships earned by students in system have risen to 16 of the 25 offered to all system in county. Employee turnover remarkably low - losses to other systems almost nil. In public relations area has successfully accomplished difficult task of pleasing public, faculty, and students during a period of constant change and multitudinous school money problems.

Responsibilities include: (1) Preparation, presentation, and enforcement of budgets. (2) Finding and hiring qualified teachers. (3) Curriculum planning and equipment procurement. (4) Overall supervision of all schools in system. (5) Contact with and follow-up on architectural planning and construction of all buildings, plus specifying and installing all new equipment. (6) Personnel Supervisor.

Reason for desiring change: Desires to leave public life.

1969–1978
SUPERVISING PRINCIPAL
As Supervising Principal was confronted with task of taking school through complex, difficult centralization procedures.

Spoke to groups of citizens at all levels; successfully solved the multiple problems which arose. Supervised planning and construction of new centralized building, as well as its ultimate operation and operating personnel.

Reason for leaving: To accept position above.

1959–1969
DIRECTOR PHYSICAL EDUCATION
Coached all athletic teams; planned all gymnasium programs. Success indicated by record of winning teams (several championships in basketball and football) in addition to outstanding record of cooperation from both students and other faculty members. Completed Masters in Education during this period; left to take supervisory position.

Amplified Resume   Stewart T. Morris

GENERAL

Activities include:

1. President of Central Zone of Michigan State Teachers' Association (10,000 teachers).

2. State Director, Michigan State Teachers' Association.

3. Chairman Michigan State Fund Raising Drive for Retired Teachers' Home.

4. Past Chairman Michigan State Teachers' Public Relations Committee.

5. Past President Rogers City Rotary Club.

6. Board of Directors of: Rogers City Savings Bank, Michigan State Public High School Athletic Association, Michigan State Public High School Athletic Protection Plan (insurance).

7. Chairman: Christmas and Easter Seal Drive, annual Red Cross Drive, Civic Music Association Drive.

8. Member Executive Committee Michigan State High School Athletic Association.

REFERENCES

Available

Synopsis of Resume of:
DOUGLAS STEWART

176 West Adams St.
Pensacola, FL 32502
Phone: (904) 537–7554

JOB OBJECTIVE

Position as Analytical Chemist

EMPLOYMENT

1977–1980   U.S. PROPELLANT PLANT, Pensacola, FL
Yearly income increased $4,800 during employment.
Aeronautical Power Plant Research Engineer (GS-11).

11/72–1977   BELMONT PROVING GROUND, Belmont, NV
Yearly income increased $3,320 during employment.
Chemist (chemical warfare installation, GS-9).

10/70–10/72   STANDARD FOODS CORP., Frankfurt, KY
(Now Div. Standard Brands Inc.)
Control Chemist. Analyzed food product samples,
plus raw materials. Tested for vitamin content,
acidity, salt, sugar, etc. Employment terminated
by standardized procedures eliminating need for chemist.

Prior   Summer employments: laborer, farm work, substitute mail carrier.

EDUCATION

1965–1969   University of Lexington, Lexington, KY
Degree: B.S. in Chemistry.
Expenses: Earned 50% of cost (approximate).
Activities: Band; business fraternity.
1970–1971   Frankfurt Institute, Frankfurt, KY
Course in Speed Reading (evening).

PERSONAL

Born: 1/6/47 in Fulton, KY. Height 6'1"; wt. 185 lbs.
Married: Wife registered nurse; no children.
Residence: Rents home; free to relocate.
Hobbies: Reading technical periodicals; music; swimming.

(FOR AMPLIFICATION PLEASE SEE FOLLOWING)
*Showing conscientious application to position beyond training, as well as honesty and frankness in reason
for leaving well-paying responsible position.*

Amplified Resume

EMPLOYMENT HIGHLIGHTS

1977–1980
U.S. PROPELLANT PLANT (Mfr's Rocket Propellants)

Transferred from Nevada installation as a Physical Chemist GS-9 to fill a position set up for a higher rated chemist. Assigned to design test procedures and supervise the work of testing materials used for rocket fuels after they had left the production line.

Required to design test equipment (some from government blueprints, others from own ideas). Visited similar naval installations to observe work done on similar materials; acted as liaison man between installations. Directly supervised 6 technicians, and many others were at his disposal.

Results: So successfully fulfilled requirements of position (supposedly beyond him), was promoted to final position and rated GS-11.

This position also beyond his training. Continued above responsibilities with added ones of designing parts of rockets and developing rocket fuels. Designed programs of tests to be accomplished. Was concerned with procuring test items and equipment, assembling test data, and the calculations to be arrived at from this data. Wrote final reports. Directed same group shown under GS-9 duties, plus calculators and other specialists. Position also required extensive outside contact with suppliers and technical personnel at other installations.

Reason for leaving: Successfully filled position requiring considerable experience outside chemistry field. Strain too great; resigned to seek more suitable position.

11/72–1977
BELMONT PROVING GROUND

Employed as General Chemist rated GS-5. Prepared solutions and assisted in laboratory analysis. Promoted after 4 months to GS-7 with essentially same work. Promoted after year and one-half to Analytical Chemist.

Supervised up to 20 personnel in actual field tests for which he designed test equipment and instruments. Transferred to laboratory, assigned to chemical research utilizing and applying information acquired in field work. (Note): much of the test equipment and many of the test procedures he designed are currently in regular use.

Reason for leaving: Requested and received transfer to southern installation.

REFERENCES AVAILABLE

Synopsis of Resume of:
KATHLEEN SNOW

45 Riverside Drive,
N.Y., NY 10024
Phone: RIverside 3—7654

JOB OBJECTIVE

Clerk - Typist

EMPLOYMENT

1979–Present   File clerk-typist, general office work.
                Goldsmith Mfg. Co. (ladies coats)
                1400 Broadway, New York, NY

1975–1979   File clerk-typist, general office work.
                Scranton Publishing Co. (books)
                400 Park Ave., New York, NY

1973–1975   Professional Dancer
                Radio City Music Hall
                Rockefeller Center, New York, NY

Prior   Part-time employment during school years included: file-clerk in
                school administration office; roles in off-Broadway plays.

EDUCATION

High School: Walton High School, Bronx, NY
                Graduated 1973
Current: Wilson Secretarial School, NYC, NY (nights)
                2 yr. secretarial course; 1 yr. completed.
                Includes: Typing, Speed Writing, Business
                Machines, Business Arithmetic, Business
                English, Basic Bookkeeping.

PERSONAL

Born: 5/10/55 in Trenton, NJ. Marital Status: single.
Appearance: Weight 120; height 5'4"
Health: Excellent.
Residence: Living with aunt; free to relocate.
Finances: No debts.
Hobbies: Tennis; dancing, records.

(FOR AMPLIFICATION PLEASE SEE FOLLOWING)

*A frequent pattern; high school graduate who has shown reliability and who wishes solid job. First person
form acceptable at this level.*

Amplified Resume

EMPLOYMENT HIGHLIGHTS

1979–Present
GOLDSMITH MFG. CO.

Types statements and correspondence; does general filing. Has been given additional responsibilities of composing portion of correspondence, plus dictaphone work. On own initiative familiarized herself with switch board operation; filled in in absence of the operator. Also did substitute modeling during sickness or vacation absence of regular models.

Indication of employer satisfaction: $10 per week merit raise after 8 mos.

Reason for desiring change: Company soon to be liquidated.

1975–1979
SCRANTON PUBLISHING CO.

Took care of inter-office communication delivery of messages; did general filing and typing; worked Verifax machines, making copies of originals. Occasionally filled in as receptionist, handling telephone calls and making appointments.

Reason for leaving: Higher salary.

1973–1975
RADIO CITY MUSIC HALL

Auditioned for position as "Rockette" following high school graduation. Was offered job; accepted.

Reason for leaving: Found it too difficult maintaining the weight requirements necessary for precision dancing; also wished to get into a more stable field.

GENERAL

Left each position on best of terms with immediate employer; has excellent references from each.

Synopsis of Resume of
SUSAN WAYNE

3978 Sandringham Drive
Atlanta, GA 30305
Phone: 233–0875

OBJECTIVE

Position in Communications that would utilize educational major
and current experience

EMPLOYMENT

1978–Present WEAT-TV, Atlanta, GA
  Assistant Traffic Director
  Camera assistant
  Talent

Part-time Sarasota Board of Education, FL
1975–1977 Classroom aide in Headstart Program.
  Maas Department Store, Sarasota, FL
  Sales, window dressing, modeling.

EDUCATION

1973–1977 Florida State University, Tallahassee, FL
  Degree:
  Bachelor of Arts.
  Major:
  Mass Communications.

PERSONAL

Age: 25 Born 1955, St. Petersburg, FL. Single.
Health: Excellent.
Appearance: Height 5′6″; weight 118.
Hobbies: Water sports; tennis; sewing, amateur theater.
Affiliations: YWCA; Community Theater; Civic Music Association.

(FOR AMPLIFICATION PLEASE SEE FOLLOWING)
*Anxious to get foot in door of larger market television studio; consequently avoided specific objective that
would narrow opportunity for being considered for any possible opening.*

Amplified Resume   Susan Wayne

EMPLOYMENT

July 1978–Present

Employed as general utility girl at station WEAT-TV. Duties consisted of general office work, filling in at receptionist's desk, filing and checking logs in the Traffic Department.

After approximately four months was promoted to position of assistant to the Traffic Director. Duties involved learning the process involved in creating a television log; procuring sales availabilities for the sales department; organization and preparation of billing information for the bookkeeping department. In addition, pulled and distributed teletype data, contacted syndicators and distributors of taped shows and films to insure proper scheduling and playdates. Prepared advanced program information for television publications.

In addition, was given responsibility for organizing the film department during interim period from resignation of film director until replacement was located. Trained the replacement in innovative film handling and shipping procedures, resulting in vastly improved, stream-lined film department.

Assisted in production of commercials, have appeared on camera for several taped commercials; have operated camera on both live and taped local shows. Have written copy and done voice-overs.

Reason for leaving:

Wish to relocate in larger market area.

REFERENCES

Available on Request

Synopsis of Resume of:
FRANK L. PALMER

23 Antlers Dr.,
Lake Bluff, IL 60044
Phone: (309) 629–5742

OBJECTIVE

Training Position in Computer Programming where education in field can be utilized.

EMPLOYMENT

1977–Present	**HYDROMETER CALIBRATOR** - Instrument Assembler. American Optical Co., Lake Bluff, IL
Prior	Part-time and summer employments prior to service. Note: been gainfully employed from early youth, financially assisting widowed mother and defraying full cost of education.

EDUCATION

1969	Hayes High School, Hayes, KS Awarded scholarship to Institute below.
1970	Wichita Institute of Technology, Wichita, KS Emphasis on college level math; left voluntarily to enter service.
1976	Burroughs Training School. Course in Computer Programming.
Service 1971–1976	U.S. Navy. Seaman Recruit to Dental Technician l/c. Honorable Discharge; no Reserve obligation.

PERSONAL

Born:	10/5/51 in Salina, KS. Height 5'8"; wt. 165 lbs.
Married:	1976; wife has B.S. in Music Education; no children.
Health:	Good; no physical limitations; last physical 1/79.
Residence:	Rents apartment; would relocate for proper opportunity.
Hobbies:	Sports in general; stamp collecting.
Affiliations:	Men's Civic Club; Lions Club; church member.

(FOR AMPLIFICATION PLEASE SEE FOLLOWING)
Resume for trainee applicant stressing self-starting qualities, among the most looked-for qualification in trainees.

Amplified Resume

EMPLOYMENT HIGHLIGHTS

1977–Present
AMERICAN OPTICAL COMPANY
Mfr. Temperature and other precision instruments.

Originally employed in sub and final assembly of various instruments; in 6 months transferred to hydrometer calibration. Works alone as sole individual in the activity. Begins with bare instrument of various sizes; uses several basic fluids at controlled temperatures, using mathematical interpolations to fit scales into tubes for proper reading with various solutions.

Except for special rush and/or emergency orders, sets own work pattern. To eliminate bottlenecks due to lack of essential supplies, has learned to operate glass tube and bulb producing machinery and, when necessary, produces own supplies.

Excellent relations with co-workers and superiors. Company's appreciation of worth indicated by increase in yearly salary of approximately $2,000.

Reason for desiring change: Has trained self for position in growing computer field; would make change (to utilize this preparation) to progressive company offering salary commensurate with ability to produce.

GENERAL

Entirely on own initiative, began and continues Burroughs Training Program for Computer Programming.

Instruction has included actual operation of various machines, as well as programming experience. Marks ranged from "A" to "B plus." Plans to continue data processing studies as employment permits.

REFERENCES

On Request

Synopsis of Resume of:
ANTHONY J. MICELLI

5007 Bristol Ave.
Sioux Falls, SD 57105
Phone: (605) 729–1062

JOB OBJECTIVE

Superintendent of Construction, or Carpenter's Superintendent

EMPLOYMENT

1/77–Present	CARPENTER (fill in position) J. Ackerman & Son, Sioux Falls, SD
6/75–12/76	GENERAL SUPERINTENDENT ($2 million apartment) Regal Homes Inc., Sioux Falls, SD
3/74–5/75	GENERAL CONSTRUCTION SUPERINTENDENT Hastings Contracting Co., Aberdeen, SD
1/73–2/74	CONSTRUCTION SUPERINTENDENT ($100,000 apartment) Lindsay Construction Co., Bismark, ND
1964–1969 1971–1973	GENERAL SUPT., CARPENTER SUPT., CARPENTER FOREMAN Blanchard Construction Co., Bismark, ND
1969–1971	SELF-EMPLOYED - home builder Pierre, SD, area.
Prior	Began work as part time laborer during high school period; served apprenticeship as carpenter with Elmer D. Smith & Sons, Cheyenne, WY

EDUCATION

High School:	Cheyenne Sr. High School, Cheyenne, WY. Graduated 1961
Other:	Served apprenticeship (above); completed all required work. Bismarck Technical School (attended nights) Blue Print Reading and Estimating.

PERSONAL

Born:	10/4/43 in Cheyenne, WY. Height 5'10"; wt. 190 lbs.
Married:	4 children, ages: 9, 7 and 2 preschool.
Health:	Excellent; no physical limitations.
Residence:	Rents home; free to relocate.
Hobbies:	Hunting, fishing, gardening.
Affiliations:	Carpenters Union, church member.

(FOR AMPLIFICATION PLEASE SEE FOLLOWING)

Field where short-term employment listing need not be avoided, for "project completed" is accepted as standard and sufficient reason for employment termination. Basic skills shown through early on-the-job training, as well as through variety of jobs satisfactorily completed. Range of supervisory capability demonstrated by cost of projects successfully completed.

Amplified Resume   Anthony J. Micelli

EMPLOYMENT HIGHLIGHTS

1/77–Present
J. ACKERMAN & SONS

   Accepted carpenter's position during interim of seeking more responsible post in line with skills and experience outlined below.

6/75–12/76
REGAL HOMES INC.

   Employed as General Superintendent of the construction of the "Skyline" apartment house, (a $2,000,000, 4-floor, 90 apartment, brick and block building with brick veneer).

   Had complete supervision of the entire operation. Directed a total of 90 workmen in all trades. Directly supervised carpenters and masons, including installation of storm and sanitary sewers. Oversaw the subcontracted work in plumbing, electrical, steel, and heating. Purchased mason materials and carpenter requirements.

   Results: Project completed 4 months ahead of schedule.
              No labor group difficulties; no repercussions.

   Reason for leaving: Work completed; no other project in work.

3/74–5/75
HASTINGS CONTRACTING CO.

   Employed as general construction superintendent. Handled such projects as: building remodeling, manhole construction, roads, water lines, etc. Had as many as 4 jobs under way simultaneously with varying number of workmen according to project requirements.

   Reason for leaving: Work completed; no new projects on hand.

1/73–2/74
LINDSAY CONSTRUCTION CO.

   Employed as Construction Superintendent directing mason and carpentry work of up to 85 men. Hired, laid off (through a foreman), the following: carpenters, masons, laborers.

   Results: Built a $1,000,000 apartment house ahead of schedule and at a profit.

   Reason for leaving: Profits not sufficient to support 6 head men; company liquidated.

(continued)

1964–1969 and 1971–1973
BLANCHARD CONSTRUCTION CO.

Employed as carpenter; in 3 years promoted to Carpenter Foreman. From that point alternated as General Superintendent or Carpenter Foreman, depending on size of job, or state of other work in process.

Worked on a variety of projects, usually as man charged with responsibility of getting work underway; shifted to next project as it came along. Among major construction which he started were the following:

Greenvale Junior College - $2 million
Mandan, ND
General Foreman

Marshall Junior High - $1 million
Bismarck, ND
Foreman

Wilton Motel - $250,000
Wilton, ND
General Foreman

Reason for leaving: Left in 1969 to go into business for himself; left in 1969 to accept good offer from Lindsay Construction Co.

1969–1971
SELF-EMPLOYED HOME BUILDER

Subcontracted all but carpenter work; hired and directed that work. Earned reasonably good livelihood; however scarcity of available skilled workmen, and excellent offer to return to Blanchard (above), results in decision to terminate operations.

REFERENCES

Present, or any former employer may be contacted.

Synopsis of Resume of:
SHERMAN T. CONKLIN

542 Langley Rd.
Great Falls, MT 59401
Phone: (406) 781−8664

JOB OBJECTIVE

General Contractor

EXPERIENCE

1974−Present	Self employed - General Contractor Conklin & Son Construction Company, Great Falls, MT
1968−1974	Self employed - General Contractor Partnership, Casper, WY.
1955−1966	Miscellaneous employments in Cheyenne, WY: milling machine operator, operator heavy highway equipment, construction work (mason, carpenter). Left to attend Haxton Institute (see Education).

EDUCATION

1966−1968	Haxton Institute, Olympia, WA. Full time 2 year course in Building Construction. Graduated 3rd in class of 47.
1967−1968	International Correspondence School Architectural Course.
1970−1972	Casper High School, Casper, WY. Adult Education courses in Real Estate Appraisal, Business Law, Accounting (nights).
1968	Eastern Montana College of Education, Billings, MT Advanced Course for Home Builders. (Summer Session).
Misc:	Builders Management Seminars: attended 2 in Olympia, WA., 3 in San Francisco, 2 in Chicago, 1 in NY.
Current:	Continuous self study (technical periodicals, etc.)

PERSONAL

Born:	4/19/40 in Fort Custer, MT. Married. Height 6'; weight 195 lbs.
Health:	Excellent; no physical limitations.
Residence:	Owns home; will relocate within state.
Affiliations:	Great Falls Home Builders Association.

(FOR AMPLIFICATION PLEASE SEE FOLLOWING)

Multiple educational courses listed in detail on synopsis sheet to gain full, favorable impact of continual efforts to add to, and acquire, current know-how. Amplification has slight sales-public relations slant so that resume can be used in field other than listed under job objectives.

EXPERIENCE

SELF EMPLOYED

1968–1972

Following completion of Haxton Institute formed partnership in Casper, WY, employing about 10 personnel to take painting contracts. Continued painting activities, expanding to include mason and carpenter contracting. Profitable operation; sold out to partner to go into business with own son.

1972

Formed own business in Great Falls, MT, a faster growing area, subcontracting for various developers. Had up to 50 employees on weekly payroll. Also construction superintendent for community center project.

1973

Expanded business to include small commercial, sewer, water line work, building, electrical, carpentry and masonry.

1974–Present

Became General Contractor. Builds standard homes and small commercial buildings. Contracts range from $10,000 to $100,000. Does own sewer and water line work, masonry, plumbing, carpentry and painting.

Personally does all selling (is licensed real estate salesman). Contracts architects, brokers, finance officers of lending institutions, and prospective clients. Does all estimating (has consistently been within 1 to 2%). Is familiar with mortgage procedures, bank lending, real estate codes, building codes, and has had up to 10 projects underway simultaneously in different locations.

To assist in proper building, developed a plan or estimate sheet which has been discussed and favorably commented upon by other builders. Maintains a flow sheet of work progress indicating materials and money required at estimated times.

Gets along well with workers, many of whom have been employed by him since business was formed. Is highly regarded by local officials, and is at home dealing with authority at all levels.

Reason for desiring change:
Feels he has progressed as far as possible under existing set up. Has no time to assume the additional responsibilities necessary for expansion.

REFERENCES

Available

Synopsis of Resume of:
GORDON T. WAGNER

84 Weling Ave.
Richmond, VA 23225
Phone: (703) 262–4876

JOB OBJECTIVE

Credit Supervision

EMPLOYMENT

7/72–Present   BURLINGTON TEXTILES INC. (2000 plus emp.)
Richmond, VA
    Assistant Credit Manager

8/68–6/72   CONSOLIDATED FOODS INC. (1,000 emp.)
Elizabeth City, VA
    Credit Manager

Prior   Part time during college period & summers:
    Milo Manse, CPA, Palo Alto, CA

EDUCATION

Edison High School, Austin, TX
    President Student Council Jr. & Sr. years.
Service - USAF. Hon. Discharge
    CCA Airways Traffic Control School.
    Graduated as Traffic Controller.
9/63–6/68   Stanford University, Palo Alto, CA
    Degree: B.S. in Business Admin. Major: Acctng.
    Honors: Graduated Cum Laude.
    Expenses: Earned all over G.I. Bill.
    Activities: Debating Team: Honorary Business Fraternity.
Miscellaneous   University of Richmond, Richmond, VA
    Course sponsored by National Credit Foundation.

PERSONAL

Born: 6/5/41 in Austin, TX. Widower; no dependents.
Appearance: Height 5′8″; wt. 162. Health: excellent.
Residence: Owns home; will relocate for proper opportunity.
Hobbies: Skeet; horseback riding.
Affiliations: National Association of Credit Men; Nat. Rifle Association.
Civic: Volunteers accounting services to sundry civic organizations.

(FOR AMPLIFICATION PLEASE SEE FOLLOWING)
Both major employments for nationally known companies; therefore, company name given precedence over position title. Rather than divulge company figures, applicant shows results of effort company evaluation as indicated by salary more than doubling during employment.

Amplified Resume   Gordon T. Wagner

EMPLOYMENT

7/72–Present
BURLINGTON TEXTILES INC.

Employed in present capacity to assume full authority in extension of credit and supplemental handling of a substantial portion of company's prospective and actual accounts. Total credit in substantial 7 figures. Accounts made up of textile wholesalers and are located throughout the entire United States, Canada, Mexico and South America. Consequently, thorough knowledge of foreign as well as domestic credit problems is required and essential.

Grants credit on basis of financial statements, and past credit record. For single accounts, amounts often reach figures exceeding customers' net worth. Representing so major a creditor necessitates his acting as advisor to the customer firm or business on policies and procedures. Results of this assistance have proved so successful, his advice is constantly sought and readily accepted.

Supervise 10 members of credit department in details of credit work; has full authority when accounts become delinquent. Works closely with sales force; prospects for likely accounts which are suggested to sales. Notifies salesman of trouble areas; as credit is geared to assist, not hamper, sales by excessive caution, sound judgment is required.

In general, develops special approaches to trouble areas. Knows and is known to management of hundreds of companies throughout North and South America. Has met his company's requirements in all respects as shown by his salary more than doubling during this employment.

Reason for desiring change: Wants top credit spot not probable in present company for several years.

8/68–6/72
CONSOLIDATED FOODS INC.

Employed as Credit Clerk, promoted to Assistant Credit Manager to Credit Manager.

Work and responsibilities similar to above on smaller scale. Accounts (all domestic), included: jobbers, distributors, wholesale groceries.

Reason for leaving: To accept better paying position, and to broaden experience with larger company above.

REFERENCES

Available

Synopsis of Resume of:
BRUCE R. SHEAHAN

87 Kenwood Ave.
New Orleans, LA 70150
Phone: (504) 239–1063

JOB OBJECTIVE

Position in Customer Service or Sales Field

EMPLOYMENT

1974–12/79	**MANAGER MARKETING ADMINISTRATION** Apex Equipment Sales Inc., New Orleans, LA
1969–1974	**CUSTOMER SERVICE MAN** Altex Fixture Inc., Baton Rouge, LA
1966–1969	**SALESMAN** Morris Sales and Service Co., Hot Springs, AR
1962–1966	**SALESMAN** Brock-Hall Food Co., Hot Springs, AR Route salesman: resigned to accept better position.
Prior service	Little Rock, AR: American Petroleum Co. - shipping clerk. 1961–1962 Allstate Insurance Co. - salesman. 1960–1961

EDUCATION

College:	Little Rock University, Little Rock, AR Evening School. 1960–1966 Business Administration course of study.
Other:	Company sponsored sales training courses. Correspondence course in Accounting (current).

SERVICE

1957–1960	U.S. Navy. Apprentice Seaman to Petty Officer 3/c. Served in Pacific Theater in invasions of Kwajalein, Midway, Phillippines. Hon. Discharge; not in Reserve.

PERSONAL

Born:	6/11/39 in Little Rock, AR. Height 6'; wt. 190 lbs.
Married:	Wife attended Arkansas State Teachers' College. Three children.
Health:	Excellent.
Affiliations:	Sales Executives Club of New Orleans; Rotary International.

(FOR AMPLIFICATION PLEASE SEE FOLLOWING)

Qualifications for present job objective given focus by position titles on synopsis sheet, and credibility is indicated through amplified details. General summary added to point up good overall record, lacking in specific major accomplishments.

Amplified Resume   Bruce R. Sheahan

EMPLOYMENT HIGHLIGHTS

1974–12/79
APEX EQUIPMENT SALES INC.
(Mfrs.: dental, surgical, laboratory equipment)

Employed originally to assist the manager of dental equipment sales section, as well as replace him during yearly monthly vacations and regular trip absences.

Handled all customer correspondence, all inside customer contact by phone or plant visitation. Had all dental equipment orders properly entered and routed through plant. Maintained regular contact with 25 representatives throughout the southwest.

Retained position throughout transition period following sale of company to present owners (3/79). Promoted to newly created position of Manager of Marketing Administration supervising 8 personnel in processing all orders entering plant for all products. Yearly dollar volume: low 8 figures.

Handled all customer correspondence; revised order handling procedure, resulting in substantial reduction in order handling costs.

Reason for leaving: New ownership resulted in frequent policy and personnel changes, creating atmosphere of impermanence. Recent promotion added responsibility with no monetary increase. Submitted resignation 12/79. Has agreed to remain for short period (not exceeding 3 months) to assist in training replacement. Currently available for interview.

1969–1974
ALTEX FIXTURE INC.
(Wood and Plastic display equipment)

Employed as Sales Trainee and Apprentice to Sales Engineer. Moved directly into customer sales department with full charge of all order details on repair of returned or defective goods and parts replacement. Remained in same capacity throughout employment, and was retained despite drastic cut in company sales force.

Reason for leaving: To accept better position above.

1966–1969
MORRIS SALES & SERVICE CO.
(Distributors offset and letter press machines & equipment)

Employed as salesman to cover Hot Springs, AR and 6 country surrounding area. Called on printers and such industrial and commercial firms as might be prospective customers. Business was new. All prospects had to be located, and volume built from zero.

Earned reasonably good income from commission sales to substantial, sound firms; however, as duplicating machines are in "long life" category, repeat sales were unlikely.

Reason for leaving: Resigned to seek position offering better opportunity to build volume.

GENERAL

Record shows outside and inside sales experience; ability to supervise and develop new and/or expand old departments. Ability to meet public, get along with co-workers, earn respect of superiors.

REFERENCES

Available

Synopsis of Resume of:
ARNOLD BAXTER

110 Summer St.
Los Angeles, CA 90057
Phone: (213) 542–2114

JOB OBJECTIVE

Department Supervisor

EMPLOYMENT

1974–Present   HILL MANUFACTURING CO.
874 Castile St., Los Angeles, CA
IBM Supervisor

1966–1974   SAUDI OIL COMPANY, 302 Madison Ave., New York, NY
Computer Operator in Dhahran, Saudi Arabia.

1959–1966   SHELL CHEMICAL CORP., Newark, NJ
(service   Computer Operator
interrupted)   (Moved up from stock boy)

1959   LITTLESTONE STEEL CO., Hamilton, Ontario, Canada
Miscellaneous duties (part time and summer employment)

EDUCATION

Jefferson High School, Winnetka, IL
Graduated. (Early high school in Hamilton, Ontario.)
Reid Institute (correspondence), New York, NY. Incomplete.
1974–1978   Alenmard Technical Institute, Los Angeles, CA
Night courses in: Accounting, Industrial Mgmt.,
Office and Personnel Mgmt. Diploma.
Current: Company sponsored course in "Time and Motion Study.

PERSONAL

Age: 33   Born 7/2/47 in Chicago, IL. Marital status: single.
Health: Good; Height 5'11"; weight 204 lbs.
Residence: Rents apartment; free to relocate.
Hobbies: Football (participation and spectator); self education.
Affiliations: American Machine Accounting Association; C. of C.

(FOR AMPLIFICATION PLEASE SEE FOLLOWING)
Company name given precedence over position title, as companies are well known. This gives position added importance, indicating larger operation responsibility. In lieu of formal education, determination for self-education emphasized.

Amplified Resume   Arnold Baxter

EMPLOYMENT HIGHLIGHTS

1974–Present
HILL MANUFACTURING CO.
(Industrial textile, interior trim)

Originally employed as Computer Operator. Department composed of 15 persons (including time recording clerks); was inefficiently run. In 6 weeks was promoted to Supervisor of the Department, and directed to bring it into full usefulness.

Replaced obsolete machines, eliminating 2 verifyers, reduced his work force from 15 to 10. Retrained the entire group, replaced unsuitable personnel, hired more effective operators.

Reduced force handles 43 applications including: Accounts Receivable and Payable, Payroll, Labor Analysis, Cost of Sales, Inventory Control, Customer Mailings, Reports, all time recording operations.

Company operations have increased over 28%; over 450 personnel are employed; branch has been added in Canada; one is in formation in the East. Computer work for branch plants, as well as main plant, is performed in Los Angeles. Operation is smooth, employee relations good. Only reason for change would be to take over a larger operation. Yearly income has increased by over $14,700 since 1974.

1966–1974
SAUDI OIL COMPANY

Employed on four year contract as Computer Operator in Saudi Arabia, a major installation with all types of equipment up to computers. Moved up to supervision of material order and supply system for his district. This meant a weekly balance of all items received by the district. Contract renewed for second four year period. Resigned after completion of second contract to return to normal living conditions.

1959–1966
SHELL CHEMICAL CORP.

Employed as stock boy until entering service. Returned in same capacity; took leave of absence to complete high school. Returned as Computer Operator; operated all types of equipment until resigned in 1966 to accept highly paid overseas position.

CONCLUSION

Over 15 years of computer experience; last 10 in positions of responsibility. Fully qualified on all equipment up to computer. Consistently good record in obtaining maximum from personnel, while maintaining good-will.

Synopsis of Resume of:
PAUL S. BERKMAN

364 Hillside Dr.
Arlington, VA 22218
Phone: (703) 227–9842

OBJECTIVE

Position in Data Processing Field leading to Programming.

EMPLOYMENT

1976–Present	Mortgage Specialist (Data Processing Department) Marine National Bank, Arlington, VA
Prior	School period employments:

Clark's Garage, Henderson, NC
   Station attendant.
Campus custodian.
   Henderson Technical U., Henderson, NC
Deliveryman - truck driver.
   Bailey Dairy, Knoxville, TN

EDUCATION

1972–1975	Henderson Technical University, Henderson, NC 3-year Business Program. Diploma. Emphasis: office management, data processing.
1976	Company sponsored course in Computer Programming.

PERSONAL

Born:	2/3/53 in Knoxville, TN. Height 6'; wt. 185 lbs. Married.
Health:	Excellent; no physical limitations.
Residence:	Rents apartment; free to relocate.
Hobbies:	Antique cars; hunting; fishing.
Affiliations:	National Rifle Association; church member.

(FOR AMPLIFICATION PLEASE SEE FOLLOWING)
Emphasis on competency in chosen field pointing up increased qualification for more responsible post in same field.

EMPLOYMENT DETAILS

1976–Present
MARINE NATIONAL BANK
(Large commercial bank - multiple branches)

Completed training period in one month (as against an average of two months); assigned to Personal Loan Dept. as computer operator.

Responsible for development of data proving personal loans daily against bank general ledger. Made daily adjustments to maintain up-to-date records. Developed monthly reports on Loan Department activities, demonstrating increases in loan volume, profitability, etc.

At own request, and to broaden experience in bank data processing, was granted transfer to computer processing of mortgages (home and business).

Maintains computer record of all mortgages accepted, on file, and paid off; all payments, delinquencies and changes. Prepares monthly reports on various phases of department operations as requested by management. Develops monthly listing of delinquencies for action by proper personnel.

Equipment operated includes: collators, sorters, key punches, interpreters, accounting machines. As daily tasks are widely diversified, thorough knowledge of equipment is required, as well as wide range of skills and abilities.

Reason for desiring change:

Job is secure; relation with superiors and co-workers is excellent. However, opportunity for real progress and/or substantially increased income appears limited. Immediate superior concurs and has volunteered excellent reference.

REFERENCES

On Request

Resume of:
ANDREA CUMMINGS

752 Sherwood Ave.
Sharon, CN 06069
Phone: (203) 643−7792

JOB OBJECTIVE

Position in Sales and/or Demonstrating.

EMPLOYMENT

10/79−4/80
Demonstrator
Ward Baking Company
29 Clincon Ave., Sharon, CN

Employed as one of four in area to demonstrate and promote sale of special bakery items (for example, bake-and-serve type rolls), as well as standard production items (bread, pastries, etc.).

With special equipment (oven, etc.), was transported to store selected for day's effort. Stores were located in small towns surrounding the Sharon, Conn. area; were of varying size and type, consequently had widely varying clientele.

At demonstration worked alone, personally baking most items and offering samples to customers. After samples were consumed, it was her responsibility to solicit opinions on the items, and suggest purchase of similar ones. Was expected to sell stock of merchandise which accompanied demonstration, and at same time make an impression that would reflect favorably on company and store.

Results

1. Gave full employer-satisfaction. Maintained good volume of merchandise sale where possible (on occasion, store did so little business there were no customers to approach).

2. Gained valuable experience in handling persons of all nationalities, age groups, and walks of life. Learned value of a smile and courtesy; became knowledgeable in evaluating and handling prospects.

Reason for leaving:

Involved in automobile accident; was replaced, of necessity, during convalescence.

(FOR AMPLIFICATION PLEASE SEE FOLLOWING)
Minor level responsibility employment given added stature through major detail. Lack of formal education de-emphasized through generalization of educational detail.

Andrea Cummings

EMPLOYMENT
(continued)

10/78–9/79
Waitress

Old Spain Restaurant, Sharon, CN. Quality restaurant catering to women luncheon trade. Gained experience in meeting and dealing with public as well as handling money and coping with sundry problems posed by diners. Left to accept better position with Ward.

1/77–10/78
Sales Clerk

Hendricks (stationery store), Bridgeport, CN. Employed as temporary clerk during special promotion; record was such was offered and accepted permanent position.

Began in card and stationery department. Promoted to office equipment department, selling such costly equipment as desks, files, etc. Had regular contact with business and executive personnel; required good knowledge of items offered as well as proper technique to consummate sale. Left when family moved.

1974–1976
Part time sales

Sundry part time sales clerk positions during high school period.
Sold: houseware items, women's dresses, garden supplies.

EDUCATION

Formal
Bridgeport, CN, public schools.
Special Training
Demonstration Training Course given by Ward Baking
Co. General training in all phases of store operation
gained in multiple store employment.

Note: Would enter training program if requisite to employment.

PERSONAL

Born: 9/2/58 in Bridgeport, CN. Marital status: single.
Appearance: Height 5'2"; Weight 118 lbs.
Residence: Rents apartment; free to relocate.
Health: Excellent; has fully recuperated from accident.
Hobbies: Dancing; Cooking.
General: Speaks with authority in well modulated tones;
                 good presence and command of English.

(All former employers may be contacted for reference)

Synopsis of Resume of:
DOROTHY L. HOPKINS

603 Murray St.
Little Rock, AR 72219
Phone: (501) 371–1832

JOB OBJECTIVE

Dental Hygienist in Periodontal Field

EDUCATION

1969
University of Tennessee, Memphis, Tenn.
College of Dentistry - School of Dental Hygiene. Graduated.

Other:
Hendrix College, Conway, Arkansas. Graduated 1957.

Continuing workshops in special areas to fulfill requirements of dental hygienist license renewal.

EMPLOYMENT

1970–Present
George A. Johnson, D.D.S. - Periodontist.
900 W. Markan St., Little Rock, Arkansas.
  Dental Hygienist in office with 4 full-time and 3 part-time employees.

1969–1970
Wallace Fowler, D.D.S. - General Practice.
  Dental Hygienist.

Prior
Part-time positions as dental hygienist following marriage in 1959.

PERSONAL

Born: 1935. Married; children self-supporting. Owns home and car.
Health: Good. Height 5'10"; wt. 140 lbs.
Hobbies: Gardening; tennis; home do-it-yourself projects.
Affiliations: American Dental Hygiene Society.

(FOR AMPLIFICATION PLEASE SEE FOLLOWING)

Divorced woman who has remarried with "his and her" children, but all self-supporting. Better than average education in her field, thus it appears ahead of employment. Amplification stresses experience and dependability.

Amplified Resume   Dorothy L. Hopkins

EXPERIENCE

1970–Present
GEO. A. JOHNSON, D.D.S. - PERIODONTIST

As highly skilled, experienced hygienist in the office of one of the area's leading periodontists, has myriad duties of specialized nature performed without supervision.

Performs oral prophylaxis, as well as some root planing and curettage. Places and removes periodontal dressings; gives post operative instructions. Takes blood pressure readings; takes and develops x-rays.

Charts mouths; does cavity and oral cancer surveys. Does fluoride treatments; takes patient histories.

Percentage of time is devoted to patient education. Involves: staining teeth to reveal plaque; pointing out presence of plaque; emphasizing and demonstrating proper brushing and flossing techniques and importance of regular home-care.

Reason for change:
Dr. Johnson is retiring. He may be contacted for reference. His letter of reference states in part, "Mrs. Hopkins is my dependable right-hand man and my patients love her."

1969–1970
WALLACE FOWLER, D.D.S. - General Practice

Following divorce in 1968, accepted position as dental hygienist performing standard functions: prophylaxis; charted patient's mouths; did cavity surveys; took and developed x-rays; confirmed and made appointments.

Left to accept position in preferred periodontal field.

REFERENCES

On request

Synopsis of Resume of:
HUGH STELJES

120 Farley St.,
Indianapolis, IN 46241
Phone: (317) 611–9044

JOB OBJECTIVE

Position in Drafting - Supervision - or leading to it.

EMPLOYMENT

1/73–Present

DRAFTSMAN I
Electronic Communications Inc.,
200 Front St., Indianapolis, IN

1967–12/72

School period employment (part time and summers):
Ace Vending Machine Co., Jefferson City, MO
Employed by District Mgr., repaired machines at home.

Between school period employment (full time):
Miller Parts & Equipment Co., Jefferson City, MO
Repaired heavy equipment (tractors, industrial equip., etc.)
Offered substantial raise to remain; resigned to utilize education.

EDUCATION

1967–1970

Salem High School, Salem, MO
Jefferson City High School, Jefferson City, MO
Took drafting; completed 2 years credit in
Architectural Drafting.

1970–1972

Bates Technical Institute, Jefferson City, MO
Evening courses in: Basic Electronics, Descriptive
Geometry, Trigonometry, Drafting.

PERSONAL

Born: 1/21/52 in Salem, MO. Marital status: single.
Appearance: Height 5'7½"; weight 165 lbs.
Health: Excellent; no physical limitations; last physical 1979.
Residence: Boards with relatives; free to relocate.
Hobbies: Music (plays piano); do-it-yourself repair projects.
Affiliations: YMCA.

(FOR AMPLIFICATION SEE FOLLOWING)
One-job work history requiring thorough coverage to expose all capabilities.

Amplified Resume   Hugh Steljes

EMPLOYMENT

1/73–Present
ELECTRONIC COMMUNICATIONS INC.

Employed originally as Draftsman III. Learned company systems; handled small detail drawings, electrical and mechanical.

In two years moved up to Class II. Prepared fabrication or detail drawings required for manufacturing purposes. Worked with designers and engineers under minimum supervision. Also worked from engineering sketches, designs or layouts.

Was (and is) frequently given a rough sketch of a part or assembly of parts with only main or overall dimensions specified. Required to locate tubes, switches, other electronic or mechanical parts, actually design package. Makes detail drawings of each element using dimensions drawn from company tolerances and engineering specifications, keeping whole package within overall dimensions required.

January 1976 was selected for and assigned to a group of Design Engineers as lead draftsman for specification control and procurement outline drawings coverage on a multi-million dollar "NIKE ZEUS" missile project. Required to be familiar with Ordnance, Bell Telephone, and General Electric Corporation systems of drawing and procedures. Has at his disposal, and is familiar with, information on vendor items available for purchase. Is authorized to select parts or units which fit overall specifications. Is given almost full responsibility for this type of mechanical item (frequently electronic or electrical.)

Makes drawings of parts to be purchased; handles correspondence with vendors. Also handles correspondence with Ordnance and Contract Associates on matters pertaining to specifications. Has become particularly expert in government procedures and specifications.

Promoted to Draftsman I during above assignment (was performing duties associated with this classification from its inception). Is now designing small units while continuing aforementioned responsibilities.

Reason for desiring change:

Better opportunity for advancement; more varied experience.

REFERENCES

Available

Resume of:
DAVID E. CLINTON

80 Brett St.,
Seattle, WA 98101
Phone: (206) 743–7635

OBJECTIVE

Position in field of Electronic Design or Drafting.

EMPLOYMENT RECORD

1975–Present   ELECTRONIC DRAFTSMAN (Design)
Farrel Photo Inc., Seattle, WA

1964–1975   Note:
Employments listed below are all project type; it is standard
procedure for crews to be broken up upon successful completion of
project.

DRAFTSMAN (electrical and mechanical)
National Electronics, Phoenix, AZ
Victor Design, Inc., Farmington, NM
Standard Products Inc., Santa Barbara, CA
Morris Electronics, Los Angeles, CA
Milo Corp., Barstow, CA
Simco Electric Co., Tucson, AZ
Western Conductor Sales, Spokane, WA
Burns Electronics, Burns, OR

EDUCATION

1959–1964   Following high school graduation, has taken variety of courses
whenever time and employment permitted.
They include: Basic Engineering, Mechanical Drawing and
Engineering, Mathematics and Physics for Mechanical Engineering,
Electronics.

PERSONAL

Born: 5/19/41 in Tucson, AZ. Height 5'10"; wt. 160 lbs. Single.
Residence: Rents; free to relocate; willing to travel; would accept overseas post.
Health: Excellent; no physical limitations; last physical 2/80.
Hobbies: Bowling; hunting; fishing.

(FOR AMPLIFICATION SEE FOLLOWING)
*Demonstrating project, or short-term employment technique, combining for clarity, listing for credulity,
giving logical reason for extraordinary number of job changes.*

Amplified Resume   Page 2

EMPLOYMENT HIGHLIGHTS

1975–Present

Farrel Photo Inc. (350 employees)
Mfr's. photographic and microfilming apparatus.

Responsible for design, layout and detailing of schematics and wiring diagrams for sundry devices produced for IBM, U.S. Army and U.S. Navy. Equipment is highly intricate; includes panel boards providing selectivity in choice of film, number of duplications and other variations, by push button. Contracts slated for completion May, 1980; has been offered future assignment not in desired field; declined.

1964–1975 Project Assignments:

National Electronics
Large manufacturer of electronic devices. Worked with company engineers and draftsmen in layout and design of classified equipment to be used in the early warning and missile systems.

Victor Design, Inc.
Major manufacturer of air conditioning equipment. Did design and layout of electrical wiring for commercial production.

Standard Products Inc.
Manufacturer heavy duty machine tools. Assisted in mechanical design and layout of extrusion presses.

Morris Electronics
Manufacturers crossbar switches, scanners, monitors. Assigned to design and layout of electronic devices.

Milo Corp./Simco Electric Co./Western Conductor Sales
Manufacturers portable & mobile testing equipment for missile and aircraft industries; manufacturers electronic components for missile, aircraft, radio, and television industries.

In above employments, duties involved: layout, design of electro-mechanical parts and devices for ground support of drone target planes, plus modernization of obsolete drawings, pictorial views of components for mechanical and electrical parts lists.

Burns Electronics
Manufacturers missiles and component parts. Revised old drawings, detailed new layouts. Did schematics, wiring diagrams, pictorial drawings, electrical parts lists, wire lists; detailed instrument panels.

REFERENCES ON REQUEST

Synopsis of Resume of:
DONALD FREER

27 Meigs St.
Olympia, WA 98501
Phone: (507) 366–3228

JOB OBJECTIVE

Field of electronics on technician level with opportunity to move up.

EMPLOYMENT

1976–Present	MANVILLE-FORBES CO., Portland, OR Service engineer for North America. Note: Continuation of employment next below: company sold out to Manville-Forbes Co.
1975–1976	ACE AUTOMATION CO., Culver City, CA Service Manager.
1959–1975	BORGMAN CORPORATION, Sacramento, CA Supervisor of mechanical maintenance.
1951–1959	KELLER FORD AGENCY, Carson City, NV Auto mechanic plus all radio repair.
1948–1950	U.S. FORESTRY SERVICE Mechanic supervising repair of road building equipment. Left to seek position in industry.
General:	Can operate or repair any type of machine in a standard machine shop.

EDUCATION

Formal:	Franklin Technical Institute, Geyser, NV Machine Design. Graduated. Culver Institute of Technology: (Evening Course) Sacramento, CA: Industrial Management.
Other:	LaSalle Technical Institute (Correspondence) NYC, NY: Radio and Electronics. Extensive home study in electricity & electronics.

PERSONAL

Born:	5/4/29 in Geyser, NV. Height 5'11"; wt. 180. Health: Good.
Married:	Wife graduate U.C.L.A.; 2 children, 1 married, 1 in college.
Residence:	Rent home; free to relocate.
Hobbies:	Hunting; fishing; model railroading.

(FOR AMPLIFICATION SEE FOLLOWING)

*Demonstrating experience equivalent accepted by many employers in lieu of college. Steady position climb
clearly indicates conscientious application of on-the-job acquired knowledge.*

Amplified Resume   Donald Freer

EMPLOYMENT HIGHLIGHTS

1976–Present
MANVILLE-FORBES CO. and
ACE AUTOMATION CO.

Employed originally by Ace Automation Co. (1976) to service and install electrically operated continuous weighing systems produced by the company.

In 1977 company sold out to Manville-Forbes Co. Company retained and ultimately promoted him to Service Engineer for all of North America. Installations run into high six figures. He supervises each one; trains service men in the local Manville-Forbes offices, in all aspects of repair and service.

Results:
Has accomplished his installations and training programs to the complete satisfaction of customers and company. Has outstanding record of no complaints - no record of faulty installations or poor service.

Reason for desiring change: Vast territory requires absence from home for several months at a time. Would change to a position permitting more time with family.

1959–1975
BORGMAN CORPORATION

Employed as one of 10 maintenance machinists repairing all types of machine shop equipment.

1966 promoted to Supervisor of Maintenance of Mechanical Equipment with up to 15 personnel under his direction. Was charged with responsibility of keeping machinery and vehicles running in a plant employing from 1500 in slow periods, to 2000 at peak, on each shift. Machinery ranged from simple machine shop devices to highly complicated special machines. For example, electrical or mechanical equipment used in modern medical laboratories.

Interviewed and recommended employment of his assistants; discharged when necessary. Trained his people when skilled men were not available. Relations with men excellent, with low turnover. Separations normally occurred as a result of company's fluctuating volume.

Has excellent letters of reference attesting to leadership ability specifically emphasizing consistently good record of turning untrained and/or poor workmen into good producers.

(continued)

Amplified Resume   Donald Freer

BORGMAN CORPORATION employment continued

Special Accomplishments

1. Developed a preventive maintenance program substantially reducing down time for machines, with corresponding saving for company.

2. Wrote training manual still in use by company.

Reason for change: In drastic economy move, departments consolidated and position abolished. Asked to remain in position of lesser responsibility and at lower salary; elected to resign.

REFERENCES

Available on Request. Please no contact with present company
until after interview.

Synopsis of Resume of:
HAROLD KNOWLAND

876 Highland Drive,
Seattle, WA 98013
Phone: (206) 972–8762

JOB OBJECTIVE

Design Engineering in Electro-Mechanical field.

EMPLOYMENT

4/75-Present GENERAL PACIFIC INC., Seattle, WA
Income has increased by $4,850 since joining company
Machine designer.

1974–1975 DELCO ENGINEERING CO., Boise, ID
Contract design work.

1972–1974 ALLSTATE TOOL MACHINE CO., Silver City, ID
Detailer. Actual work was in electro-mech. design.

1968–1972 FOTEX INC., Silver City, ID
Draftsman

Prior Please see amplification.

EDUCATION

1953–1956 University of Southern California
Degree: 3 year's study toward BS in ME.
Compelled to leave for reasons of health.

1958–1960 Silver Springs Institute of Technology, Silver City, ID
Associate degree in design engineering,
acquired through night school attendance.

1971–1972 Company-sponsored course on "Automation."

PERSONAL

Born: 10/10/35 in Carson City, NV. Height 5'11"; weight 175 lbs.
Married: Wife attended business college; 1 son in college.
Residence: Owns home; will relocate.
Hobbies: Do-it-yourself home projects; hi-fi.
Affiliations: Allstate Society of Design Engineers.

(FOR AMPLIFICATION PLEASE SEE FOLLOWING)
Good employment record complicated by poor health factor, which cannot be ignored, but need not be dwelt upon. "Warmer climate" reason for leaving present employment is on advice of physician. Inasmuch as warmer climate will solve physical problems, it is better to limit resume geographical scope than to point up health aspect.

Amplified Resume   Harold Knowland

<h1 style="text-align:center">EMPLOYMENT HIGHLIGHTS</h1>

4/75–Present
GENERAL PACIFIC INC.
(Mechanical packings and oil seals)

Employed as machine designer in a company which requires special machines for unusual products.

Given an idea or request for a machine to perform a specific function, works out an original idea. Makes rough sketch and rough estimate. If approved, makes complete layout sketch of the device; has a detail man prepare the final drawings. Then follows through construction of device in the shop until it is put to actual production use. Has final decision on any suggested changes.

Results:
Has worked on the design of 70 machines; has completed approximately 30 since joining the company. Has had several notable successes. For example: (1) Design of impregnated packing, folding and calendering machines. (2) Machine to deliver rubber in varying plies. (3) Trimming machines for shaft seal inserts, more versatile, fast, and accurate than formerly possible.

Reason for desiring change: Warmer climate.

1968–1975
Period shows steady progression beginning with Fotex Inc., where paid as a draftsman, was doing machine design. Was offered and accepted position by Delco Engineering Co. which was expected to develop into design work.

Design aspect of position did not develop; consequently accepted offer from Allstate Tool Machine Co. Position, classified as "Detailer," gave him an opportunity to contact customers, do electro-mechanical design, including relay work. Recession caused drastic cut in work force; as last employed, was laid off. Took contract job with Delco Engineering; successfully completed.

PRIOR
Following college was employed in radio repair shop until he regained his health. (Note): after series of tests, condition correctly diagnosed as allergy; arrested and in no way impairs abilities. Was then employed by sundry firms as draftsman and detailer until 1968.

GENERAL
In recent aptitude and ability tests given by company, scored 8th of 125 working in same area.

<h2 style="text-align:center">REFERENCES</h2>

Available on request

Synopsis of Resume of:
JOHN F. PALMATIER

8074 Montgomery St.
Baltimore, MD 21211
Phone: (301) 423–1447

JOB OBJECTIVE

Position in field of electrical engineering, also experienced in electronics. Most interested in design, development or original research.

EMPLOYMENT

9/68–Present	**ELECTRICAL ENGINEER** (Patent Department) General Electronics Corp., Baltimore, MD
1/67–9/68	**SENIOR ELECTRICAL ENGINEER** Prescott Engine Inc., Richmond, VA Active on Talos Missile Launcher until company lost contract.
1954–1967	**ELECTRONIC ENGINEER** (in Micro Wave Development Group) (Moved up through various assignments). Martin Aircraft Corp., Norfolk, VA
1952–1954	**ELECTRIC POWER STATION DESIGNER** Wolf Mgmt. Engineering Co. (Consulting Engineers) New York City, NY

EDUCATION

1948–1952	Georgia School of Technology, Atlanta, GA Degree: B.S. in Electrical Engineering, including Mechanical, Hydraulic and Civil. Expenses: Tuition scholarship; earned 50% living expenses.
Misc:	Wharton School of Finance of U. of Pennsylvania Course in Economics.

PERSONAL

Born:	8/13/30 in Columbia, SC. Height 6′; wt. 195.
Married:	Wife graduate of Duke University; 2 children, ages: 13, 11.
Health:	Good; no physical limitations; last physical - 1979.
Residence:	Owns home; would relocate for proper opportunity.
Hobbies:	Tennis; family activities; Coaches Little League Baseball.
Affiliations:	Eastern Institute Electrical Engineers; Baltimore Patent Law Association; PTA.

(FOR AMPLIFICATION PLEASE SEE FOLLOWING)
Simplified presentation of long, complex record, pointing up significant projects completed. Elementary details omitted, for prospective employer in field would understand knowledge and ability implied.

Amplified Resume   John F. Palmatier

EMPLOYMENT HIGHLIGHTS

9/68–Present
GENERAL ELECTRONICS CORP.

Employed as Engineer in the Patent Department. Experienced in all phases of patent application prosecution in the electro-mechanical arts. Additionally responsible to act as consultant to Patent Counsel on all complex electronic circuit proposals including analog and digital computers, ferrite core memory systems, code communication systems, servo motor control and transistorized control circuits. Latter aspect of work required the research and design of operable circuit organizations to illustrate the electronic inventive concept.

Reason for desiring change: Increased income.

1/67–9/68
PRESCOTT ENGINE INC.

As Senior Electrical Engineer, directed the development of various control and display panels for local or remote control, for launching the "Talos Missile." Circuits included relays, servos, simulation signals, and fault finding circuits. Was responsible for estimating the cost of the whole electrical system.

Directed the work of 8 engineers and 2 technicians in the development of functional schematics and sequence charts for the system. All of the aforementioned completed before project was cancelled.

1954–1967
MARTIN AIRCRAFT CORP.

1954–1957

Employed as Engineer on Navy Receiver Project. Worked with another engineer from embryo to model stage. Then assigned as Project Engineer on what developed into a $10,000,000 contract. Completed type test of the model for final acceptance. Assisted firm of technical writers prepare instruction and maintenance manual for Navy. Project successfully completed.

1958

Project Engineer on a subcontract to GE for the third tripler and power amplifier units for an automatic tuning transmitter for Navy. Operated from 200 to 400 megacycles. Project successfully completed.

1959

Assigned to design and development of TV UHF tuner. Required design of unit, test equipment, development of production instruments and methods of test. Successfully completed.

Amplified Resume
MARTIN AIRCRAFT CORP. employment continued

John F. Palmatier

1960–1965

Engineering Supervisor of Physical Testing Laboratory. Responsible for approval testing of electronic components. Directed 17 engineers and 15 technicians in all aspects of evaluating the acceptability of all electrical components prior to purchase and final incorporation into final product.

Ordered necessary test equipment, supervised its maintenance, and designed special instruments and test setups. Had final approval of test reports. In addition, worked with purchasing and outside sales personnel when components failed to meet specifications.

1965–1967

During this period, undertook the organization of the Microwave Development Laboratory in cooperation with the department head. Primary duties included all phases of development, procurement, and evaluation of microwave equipment and testing apparatus. Five microwave links were designed and all marketed.

Reason for leaving: Better position.

REFERENCES

Available on request

Synopsis of Resume of:
HELMUT L. DAMSKY

22 Tyler Rd.
So. Providence, RI 02910
Phone: (401) 882–7664

JOB OBJECTIVE

Position in Mechanical Engineering or Design

EMPLOYMENT

1970–Present	**VICE PRESIDENT & GENERAL MANAGER** Neely Equipment Co. (Division of National Packaging Corp.) Providence, RI
1969–Present	**PLANT ENGINEER** (simultaneous with above) National Packaging Corp., Providence, RI
1965–1969	**TOOL & DIE FOREMAN** Haverhill Instruments Corp., Trenton, NJ
1962–1965	**TOOL ROOM SUPERVISOR** Elgin Machine Corp., New Haven, CT
1947–1962	Self employment in motor rebuilding during depression years; followed by varied positions in foundries, machine shops, etc.

EDUCATION

1971–1972	Providence Technical Institute, Providence, RI Course in Organic Chemistry, and Basic Radio.
1966–1968	Rhode Island College, Providence, RI (Evening Courses) Management, Economics, Mathematics.
Current:	Continuous self-study program in mechanics, engineering, electronics. Has working knowledge of Polish and German languages.

PERSONAL

Born:	8/24/28 in Poland. Naturalized citizen of U.S.
Married:	3 children, no longer dependents.
Appearance:	Height 6'; weight 210 lbs.
Health:	Excellent; no physical limitations; last physical 1979.
Hobbies:	Building hi-fi components; photography; family activities.
Affiliations:	Loyal Order of Moose; volunteer fireman.

(FOR AMPLIFICATION PLEASE SEE FOLLOWING)

Details given on major and longest employment only, to give emphasis to portion of record where important progress has been made. It is assumed prospective employer would be familiar with work involved in lesser employments; amplifications could tend to detract from impact of more recent responsibilities and accomplishments.

Amplified Resume   Helmut L. Damsky

EMPLOYMENT HIGHLIGHTS

1970–Present
Neely Equipment Co.
(Mfrs. equipment for use in printing, coating, photo-engraving,
laminating, polyethelene extrusion)

Employed originally by first parent company (Hunter Co. of Providence, R.I.), as an engineer in mechanical field. In 1971, Neely Equipment Co. was set up by the parent company; he was made General Manager. 1972 elected Vice President. Both companies became division of National Packaging Corporation in 1978.

Has all contact with prospective and established customers; discusses problems; implements solution. Makes rough sketches of machines or devices; lays out proposed production line sequence. Upon approval, makes detailed drawings and estimates. After order is obtained, supervises production of equipment, sets up in customer's plant, follows through to employee training and full customer satisfaction.

Equipment designed varies from normal mid 5 figure cost to low six figure. Photographs and sketches of successful designs created are available for inspection.

Results: Division has been profitable from start.

Reason for leaving: Greater income.

1969–Present
National Packaging Corporation

Added duties and responsibilities of Plant Engineer for National Packaging Corporation. Supervises polyethelene extrusion processes plus all mechanical and electrical maintenance.

Hires and trains groups totaling 75 personnel for these purposes. Designs and redesigns equipment for better, more efficient, quality production. Supervises rebuilding, adds controls (both electrical and mechanical) for secondhand machinery brought into plant. Has achieved quality production with these machines formerly not serviceable.

GENERAL

Record shows steady upward progression; each position left voluntarily to improve status and utilize continuing education.

REFERENCES

Available on Request

Synopsis of Resume of:
THOMAS L. LYNN

98 Brooks Ave.
Boston, MA 02646
Phone: (617) 355—9877

JOB OBJECTIVE

Engineering Technician

EMPLOYMENT

1978–Present	WFPU-TV (PBS), Boston, MA Engineering Technician.
1976–1978	Kaymart Productions, Hollywood, CA Design engineer assistant.
1975–1976	Dell Fill Productions, Beverly Hills, CA Photographer, Gaffer, Set builder.

EDUCATION

1972–1975	Boston University, Boston, MA Majored in communications with emphasis on broadcasting, production, and newswriting.
Other:	Columbia College, Hollywood, CA Courses in film production, sound recording and mixing.

PERSONAL

Born:	1954 in Columbus, OH. Parents naturalized citizens.
Married:	Wife has RN degree; no children.
Health:	Good; arrested asthmatic condition.
Finances:	Good order; rent home; free to relocate.
Hobbies:	Skiing; bridge; chess.
Affiliations:	Jaycees; Knights of Columbus.

(FOR AMPLIFICATION SEE FOLLOWING)

Amplified Resume   Thomas L. Lynn

1978–Present
WFPU-TV, Boston, MA

As engineering assistant, have been involved with production of the following:

(1) Documentary films.
(2) Weekly educational children's program.
(3) Live television coverage of centennial.

Familiar with:

(1) RCA TK-43 and RCA-44B cameras.
(2) RCA TR-70 video tape machine.
(3) RCA TCR-100 cartridge video tape machine.
(4) RCA TEP editor.
(5) Character generator.
(6) Camera and film chain; audio and video switching.
(7) Studio lighting; operation of remote equipment.
(8) Film editing.
(9) Copy writing, trailor narration, mixing, gaffing.

Reason for leaving:

Limited opportunity. Currently studying for first class radio telephone license.

Summary

All previous experience has contributed to over-all knowledge in chosen field. Has personally designed and built custom film editing equipment and projection devices, as well as custom dubbing studio.

REFERENCES

On request. Please do not contact present employer at this time.

Synopsis of Resume of:
LINDA KURTZ

155 Oakville Ave.
Rye, NY 10580
Phone: (716) 555–9862;
Home: 867–5493

JOB OBJECTIVE

Fashion Coordinator

EXPERIENCE

1977–Present	HENTLEY DEPARTMENT STORE, NY Fashion Coordinator
1976–1977	Sakowitz, Houston, TX Co-owner bridal shop.
1974–1976	Kentall Modeling School, Pittsburgh, PA Model and Teacher
1972–1974	WJZ-TV, Baltimore, MD Weather girl, television commercials
Prior	Free-lance modeling (London, Paris).

EDUCATION

1966–1970	Northwestern University
	    Major: Advertising (Business Administration)
	    Minor: Applied Arts

Other:	Fluent French; working knowledge Spanish.

PERSONAL

Born:	1948 in Colorado Springs, CO; Single; Ht. 5′8″; wt. 117
Health:	Excellent.
Finances:	Good order; owns home, car, beach property.
Hobbies:	Water sports; sculpting (clay, metal); pottery; fashion research.
Affiliations:	Art League; Red Flat Charette (Environmental Organization).

(FOR AMPLIFICATION SEE FOLLOWING)
*Heavy experience divided into major categories of fashion interest to prevent its being
clouded in the sea of detail inherent in highly detailed work of fashion consulting.*

Amplified Resume   Linda Kurtz

EMPLOYMENT

1977–Present
HENTLEY DEPARTMENT STORE

Employed as fashion coordinator for leading department store in NYC. Responsibilities are in 4 major areas and encompass the following: (1) Fashion, (2) Display, (3) Training, (4) Public Relations.

Fashion

Full responsibility for the 8 to 10 major fashion shows given annually, as well as the 25 to 30 smaller shows given in-store and at various outside community organizational functions.

Meets with organizational heads to establish time, date, theme and type of clothes. In addition, establishes financial obligations involved. Hires models, selects clothes appropriate to theme; meets with buyers as well as display to communicate needs for lighting, decoration and runway set-up.

Fits models, hires dressers to assist on day of show. Supervises rehearsals, organizes backstage activity, delivers commentary. At conclusion of show, writes vouchers for models and other related personnel, supervises return of merchandise to store and security check-in. Writes critique; evaluates gains made in increased sales and publicity.

Display

Approximately 35 in-store display changes required weekly. Chooses clothes most representative of seasonal theme, accessorizes, supervises display personnel dressing mannequins for best translation of major fashion message.

Responsible for "Front and Forward Program," a program devised to present unified look to store by having all displays, cases, and T-stands coordinated and in keeping with seasonal theme.

Training

On own initiative, inaugurated fashion training program for all ready-to-wear sales personnel. Consists of following:

(a) Department meetings. Held daily with individual departments to familiarize sales personnel with unique selling points of stock in their immediate area, as well as adjacent areas.

(b) Fashion meetings. Held bi-monthly in all fashion departments for purpose of familiarizing sales personnel with total store fashion message and inventory.

Amplified Resume   Linda Kurtz

Present employment continued

Public Relations

Organizes and supervises the several store promotional holiday breakfasts given throughout the year for customers and general public.

Organizes store's annual sewing contest. Follows entries through to final judging; does commentary and final awards show.

Does public speaking and makes personal appearances promoting and enhancing the fashion, cosmetic, and general high quality image of the Henkley Department store in New York City.

Reason for desiring change:

Would make change for salary commensurate with responsibilities.

1976–1977

As co-owner of bridal shop, assisted in the reorganization of well-located, small profit business. Acted as buyer, bridal consultant and sales manager. Responsible for many innovations, including fashion shows at local high schools, and a Spring and Fall Bridal Show at the leading local hotel. By second year sales had increased by over 50%.

Reason for leaving:
Sold interest at sizeable profit to re-locate after divorce.

Prior

Following college, traveled to Europe where applied, and was hired, as high fashion model by two leading houses in London and Paris. Did commercial photography and designer shows.

Upon return to states, was employed as television weather girl; also did sundry television commercials. Left to accept job as model and teacher at the Kentall Modeling School. Left to get married.

Summary

Has excellent letters of recommendation from all former employers; dedicated career woman aiming for the top.

REFERENCES

On request. Please no contact with present employers at this time.

Resume of:
ANDREW L. MEBANE

20 Knox Rd.
Denver, CO 80240
Phone: (303) 649–8755

OBJECTIVE

Position as Flight Officer in Commercial Aviation.

RATINGS:

Commercial, Instrument, Multi-Engine, Single Engine Land.
Aircraft flown: Cherokee 140 & 150, Astec C-2, Commanche 180.

HOURS:

Total Single Engine (261), Day Hours (211), Night Hours (19.5), Hood (38.7), Link (7.8), Multi-Engine Land (12.9), Cross Country (72), Total Instruction (95), Total Instrument (46.4).

LICENSES:

Commercial, Instrument and Multi Land—1954287
Radio Telephone Operator Permit.

EDUCATION

1972   Graduated Tucson Academy, Tucson, AZ.

1974   Tucson Technical Institute.
            Course in Mechanical Engineering.

Current: Denver Aviation School.
            Will graduate Jan. 1979 with Instructor's Rating.

PERSONAL

Age: 25   Born 1/6/56 in Pheonix, AZ. Marital status: single.
Appearance: Height 6'2"; weight 190 lbs.
Health: Excellent; first class medical.
Residence: Lives with mother; free to relocate and travel.
Hobbies: Flying; skiing; hunting.
Service: Deferred by act of Congress; father killed in service.

(FOR AMPLIFICATION PLEASE SEE FOLLOWING)
"Selling" potential in untried field by pointing up past record of ambition, drive, and desire to improve status.

Andrew L. Mebane   Page 2

EMPLOYMENT

1974–Present
SILLS DEPARTMENT STORE
Denver, CO

Employed on part-time basis while attending aviation school. Has more than tripled income since initial employment, moving from package room clerk to carpet installation. Is required to be familiar with all areas of its specialized operation including estimate, measurements, cutting, binding and installation.

Willingness to work Sundays, holidays, and in any capacity needed, has resulted in steady part-time employment, defraying full cost of schooling. Employer is aware of intention to resign upon completion of aviation school, and has volunteered excellent reference.

Prior

Been gainfully employed since grammar school in variety of part-time jobs: paper route, soda fountain clerk, gas station attendant, etc.

General Summary:

Marked ambition and desire for self-improvement manifested from early age and continues to present. Employer satisfaction in every post; has left every job voluntarily with amicable relations and re-employable status.

REFERENCES

Available

Synopsis of Resume of:
STANLEY R. MORAN

74 Atkins St.
Nashville, TN 37205
Phone: (615) 431–7651

JOB OBJECTIVE

Position in supervision on foreman level, in charge of punch
press, grinding or machine shop.

EMPLOYMENT

1973–Present except for period next below	ACE SIGNAL CORP. (over 1,000 employees) 12 Market St., Nashville, TN Foreman of Punch Press, Grinding, Gear Cutting Depts. (Presently has temporary position as tool and die maker; see amplification for details).
1975–1976	GLEASON MFG. CO. (500 employees) 300 West 50th St., Knoxville, TN Tool and Die Maker
1971–1973	Assistant manager family owned restaurant in Atlanta, GA. Profitable operation; left when restaurant was sold.

EDUCATION

High School:	Fulton Senior High School, Atlanta, GA
Other: (Nights)	Brewer Business Academy, Atlanta, GA Bookkeeping & Accounting Course. Winslow Technical Institute. Machine shop courses for apprenticeship. Tenn. Agricultural & Industrial State University. Courses included: Drafting, Blueprint Reading, Mathematics, Business Mgt., Personnel Mgmt. 1976–1979.

PERSONAL

Born:	2/24/51 in Charleston, WV. Height 5'11"; wt. 196 lbs.
Married:	2 children.
Health:	Good; no physical limitations.
Residence:	Owns home; would relocate for right opportunity.
Hobbies:	Hunting; fishing; bowling.

(FOR AMPLIFICATION SEE FOLLOWING)

*Amplified as a one-employment record to point up solid background in field of present job objective. Brief
listing of former employments adequately fulfills purpose of showing steadiness of work history.*

Amplified Resume   Stanley R. Moran

EMPLOYMENT

1973–Present (except for 75–76)
ACE SIGNAL CORP. - mfrs. signals, air
traffic, and vehicular systems and devices.

1973   Originally employed as tool crib attendant. Began and completed apprenticeship
        as machinist. Remained as machinist until 1975, when left to accept greater income
        position offered by Gleason Mfg. Co. Worked as tool and die maker, engaged in
        making parts for precision instruments until company terminated operations 6/76.

7/76   Returned to Ace Signal Corp. as a tool and die maker. Remained in that capacity
        until 1977, when company paid for complete tests of aptitudes at Tenn. State
        University Testing Center.

        Of the 8 men tested, he was selected for promotion to Foreman of the Punch Press
        Dept., consisting of: 14 operators, 5 sheet metal workers and 3 set-up men. At 3
        different periods a second shift was added, giving authority over approximately 40
        personnel at maximum.

        Utilized heavy, medium and light presses, working with steel, brass, bronze, silver
        and other metals. Work ranged from pressing heavy metal for railroad equipment
        to small high precision work for electrical devices.

        In overall departmental reorganization, the Grinding and Gear Cutting Depart-
        ments were added to his responsibilities. Grinding Department operated cylindrical,
        rotary and surface grinders; Gear Cutting Dept. was concerned with gear cutting
        and broaching.

        Did all interviewing, hiring, and training of replacement personnel. Record of ac-
        complishment during entire supervisory period shows:

        1) Work regularly completed on schedule.
        2) Low rejection record.
        3) Minimum of personnel problems brought to Grievance Committee.
        4) Minimum customer complaints.

1979   Further consolidation of departments resulted in his group being absorbed in the
        larger milling and drilling group, with a Senior Foreman taking over.

Reason for desiring change: Has remained with company on an interim basis as tool and
die maker while seeking position which would fully utilize his training, ability and experience.

REFERENCES AVAILABLE

Synopsis of Resume of:
ELLIOTT L. MUNZELL

89 Brookdale Rd.
Burlington, MA 01803
Phone: (207) 249–5908

JOB OBJECTIVE

Fund Raising Administrator

EXPERIENCE

1977–Present   ASSISTANT TO EXECUTIVE DIRECTOR of Pi Lambda Phi
Fraternity.
Liaison between chapters and national organization.

1972–1977   COORDINATOR STUDENT SERVICES, Vermont Dept. of
Education.

Other: Executive Director of Boy's Summer Camp summers.
Programming responsibilities, overall supervision 20 counselors for
800 student camp.

EDUCATION

1969–1972   University of Pennsylvania. BA.
       Major: Speech - Communication
       Extra-curricular activities: Initiated and administered marketing
organization for student-made arts and crafts. Raised funds for
building, administrative costs and promotion.
       Honors
Member Student Governing Board.
Judge - University Academic Integrity Board.

PERSONAL

Born: March 8, 1950 in Cleveland, Ohio. Height 5'11"; wt. 164.
Marital Status: Single; health - excellent. Free to relocate.
Hobbies: Public speaking; snow skiing; bridge.
Affiliations: Member Toastmasters' Club, Big Brothers, Explorers' Club.

Strengths: Ability to communicate both verbally and in writing.

(FOR AMPLIFICATION PLEASE SEE THE FOLLOWING)
*Making the most of strong academic bent of young man preparing to leave the
college campus for the real world.*

Amplified Resume   Elliott Munzell - page 2

EMPLOYMENT HIGHLIGHTS

1977–Present
ASSISTANT TO EXECUTIVE DIRECTOR

Reporting directly to Executive Director, has responsibility for administration of new chapter organization, acting as consultant to chapters for program development, financial management, fund raising and membership recruitment.

Edits alumni publication, and supervises fund raising projects. Highly visible as public speaker both at state and national level. Shares responsibility for administration and detail of annual national conventions.

Achievements: Fund raising totals increased substantially; overall pledging increased by 27%; increased chapter involvement; increased publicity and promotion; news stories in two Sunday supplements.

Plans: Change in alumni newsletter to slick magazine format, with periodic contribution envelope inserts for scholarship funds; inauguration of Speakers' Bureau.

Reason for desiring change: Anxious to move to warmer climate and for full administrator status. Executive Director who he now assists is aware of intention. Has offered full cooperation in providing ample interview trip time, and documented records of achievements.

1972–1977
COORDINATOR STUDENT SERVICES

Initially employed as co-coordinator for college student service center. Served student government groups, advisory organizations and individuals in areas of rights and responsibilities. Promoted to coordinator with full responsibility. In addition, wrote and lobbied within state legislature for a variety of student related bills, a portion of which became law. Left to accept higher paid, higher level-of-responsibility current position.

OTHER

Headed up volunteer organization to raise funds for community Little League Field House. Contacted local builders for donations of materials and services resulting in $85,000 facility built cost-free.

REFERENCES

On Request

Synopsis of Resume of:
RUTH MALLORY

Care of C. Whitney
29 Gillette St.
Richmond, VA 23234
Phone: (703) 322−6647

JOB OBJECTIVE

Position as Executive Housekeeper: hotel, motel, apartment hotel.

EXPERIENCE

1978−Present   500 room hotel located in eastern Virginia.
                  Salary $150.00 per week plus full maintenance.
                  Executive Housekeeper.

1974−1978   HOTEL WAGNER, Norfolk, VA (300 rooms)
                  Salary $125.00 per week, plus full maintenance.
                  Executive Housekeeper.

1973−1974   CHATHAM HOTEL, Virginia Beach, VA. (200 rooms)
                  Salary $450 per month (no maintenance).
                  Executive Housekeeper.

1972   SEA CHEST HOTEL, Ft. Myers, FL. (150 rooms)
                  Salary $300 per month (plus apartment).
                  Executive Housekeeper.

1970−1971   NORMANDY APT. HOTEL (75 rooms), New Orleans, LA.
                  Salary $300 per month (no maintenance).
                  Executive Housekeeper.

EDUCATION

Scholastic: In Harrington, DE.

Special Training: Murey Hotel Training Course, Washington, D.C.
                  Courses in typing and bookkeeping - Niagara Falls, Canada.

PERSONAL

Age:48   Born in Harrington, DE. Widow.
Appearance: Height 5′3″; Weight 130 lbs.
Health: Good; no physical limitations.
Hobbies: Gardening; reading.
Affiliations: Executive Housekeepers Association.

(FOR AMPLIFICATION SEE FOLLOWING)

As position title remains the same, progress is shown through increase in salary and size of establishment.
Because resume was to be widely circulated, actual name of present hotel employment has been omitted.
Mail address is that of relative rather than hotel to prevent further identification.

Amplified Resume   Ruth Mallory

EXPERIENCE

1978–Present

As Executive Housekeeper for one of the leading hotels in eastern Virginia, has staff of 62 personnel under her supervision (male, female, white, black). Interviews, hires, trains, and has full right of discharge. Assigns all work, oversees its completion. Keeps time cards, records, and issues pay checks.

Satisfactory discharge of her multiple duties has been complicated by complete re-decoration and remodeling of the 500 room hotel, begun and continued during her period of employment. Has had added responsibility of consultation and supervision of seamstress personnel, as well as deadlines to be met on rooms rented but not yet completed. Turnover in her staff has been held to a minimum, indicating her ability to maintain harmony and high morale despite trying conditions.

1974–1978 HOTEL WAGNER (staff - 40)

Executive Housekeeping functions similar to above on smaller scale, with added duties peculiar to a convention hotel. For example, tearing down bedrooms and remaking them into living rooms to accommodate convention guests was weekly routine, often as many as 18–20 per day. Found strain too great; resigned.

1973–1974 CHATHAM HOTEL (staff - 35)

Satisfactorily discharged assigned duties despite general employee strike called during her tenure. Temporary position which terminated when former housekeeper returned after leave of absence.

1972 SEA CHEST HOTEL (staff - 20)

Employed as Executive Housekeeper with standard duties, plus full charge of laundry. Employment terminated when change in management brought in complete new staff.

1970–1971 NORMANDY APARTMENT HOTEL (staff - 20)

Executive Housekeeping functions on small scale, plus doubling as evening receptionist. Left to return to Florida.

Prior

Mrs. Mallory has dealt with public in various capacities, including that of head hostess in the main dining room of the Sheraton-Brock Hotel in Niagara Falls, Canada. Successfully operated two restaurants in Florida, one with partner, one as sole owner. Sold both at profit.

SUMMARY

Record shows steady climb in salary, responsibility and size of house. Offers vast store of know-how and experience. For employer esteem, see following letters of recommendation.

(continued)

Amplified Resume   Ruth Mallory

Copies of letters of recommendation. Mrs. Mallory has
originals in her possession and may be reviewed at interview.

(1) Executive Office
    Hotel Wagner
    Norfolk, VA

    October, 1978

    To Whom it may concern:

    The bearer, Mrs. Ruth Mallory, has been in my employ here at the Wagner Hotel for
    the past four years as Executive Housekeeper.

    Having operated the Wagner Hotel for the past fifteen years, I do not hesitate in saying
    that Mrs. Mallory has been my most valuable employee during that time.

    She has shown initiative, been most cooperative, and the interests of the hotel have
    always been foremost with her. She has always been pleasant, courteous, sober and
    trustworthy. It is with extreme regret I have accepted her resignation for reasons of
    her own. However, I am happy to recommend her to any employer in a similar capacity.

                                          Signed - Henry Gibson, Jr. (Gen. Mgr.)

(2) Chatham Hotel
    Virginia Beach, VA

    Mrs. Mallory has been employed as Executive Housekeeper for one year. We have
    found Mrs. Mallory industrious, responsible, careful in following instructions, and
    eager to please both superiors and guests. She is an excellent organizer, and one whom
    employees regard with respect.

    Mrs. Mallory was hired on a temporary basis, and it is with regret we come to the
    termination of the period. I recommend her without reservation. If further information
    is desired, I would be happy to have anyone contact me personally.

                                          Signed - Alfred E. Quinn, Manager

                                  NOTE

                      Additional references available

Synopsis of Resume of: 300 Rosemoor Dr.
CLINTON L. SEYMOUR   Chicago, IL 60648
                                                         Phone: (312) 497–8745

JOB OBJECTIVE

Position in field of Industrial Relations, utilizing personnel, science, industrial, engineering and accounting background.

EMPLOYMENT

1970–Present	PERSONNEL DIRECTOR Photo Products Division (present position). Progressed through Tabulating Research, Industrial Engineering, and Inventory Control positions. Bell & Howell Co., Chicago, IL
1968–1970	Management Trainee. Two year program. Left on completion; wished to change fields. Prudential Life Insurance Co., New York, NY
1965–1968	General office work. Offered managerial training. During and after college period; resigned to accept position above. Harrison Electric Products Co., Louisville, KY

EDUCATION

1961–1965	University of Louisville, Louisville, KY
	Degrees: B.S. in Business Administration
	              B.S. in Chemistry
	Honors: Offered fellowship for graduate study;
	              finances prevented acceptance.

1970–Present	Company courses in: Industrial Engineering, MTM (Methods, Time, Measurement), Conference Leadership, Human Relations, Work Measurement.

PERSONAL

Born:	6/30/40 in Cumberland, MD. Height 5'10"; wt. 160.
Married:	Wife attended U. of Louisville; one son.
Health:	Good; no physical limitations.
Residence:	Owns home; will relocate for proper opportunity.
Hobbies:	Sailing; golf; bridge.
Affiliations:	Industrial Management Council.

(FOR AMPLIFICATION SEE FOLLOWING)
One major employment record, showing chronology of promotion, as well as increased level of responsibility through increased number of personnel involved.

Amplified Resume   Clinton L. Seymour

EMPLOYMENT

1970–Present
BELL & HOWELL CO.

1970

Employed in Tabulating Research Dept., assigned to development of IBM systems for payroll and production.

1972

Industrial Engineering Department. Assignments included office systems and methods, plant layout, production methods, and cost studies. Assignments based on accounting background included:

1. System of company gross profit shrinkage. Result: substantial reduction of loss by proper accounting methods, with major reduction in paperwork.

2. Efficiency study of cafeteria operations to minimize annual six figure loss. Result: major reduction of loss to manageable level.

3. Coordinating and directing the relocation of Industrial Engineering Dept. Involved working with construction engineers, planning and timing move sequences so as to eliminate work interruption. Completed precisely on schedule.

1974

Moved to Photo Products Division, and promoted to department head of Inventory Control. Supervised 6 separate offices with 120 personnel, whose function was preparation of payroll, production control, in-process inventory records.

Department was disorganized due to transfer of previous department head. Met challenge. Streamlined operations, handled increased work load from production increases with same work force; boosted morale.

At request of Division Superintendent, prepared special cost analysis of old payroll reporting methods compared with cost of IBM applications. Developed presentation which reached top level management.

1975

Promoted to present position of Personnel Director of Photo Products Division, with over 2,500 personnel. Handles employment of hourly workers through 3 assistants. Personally interviews and coordinates hiring of business and engineering personnel. Screens records, recommends promotions, makes decisions on upgrading.

Amplified Resume   Clinton L. Seymour

Present employment continued

Participates in solving problems involving worker grievances, job changes, absence, inadequate performance and rate adjustments. Assists in job evaluation, rate and performance reviews of all personnel, and in division organization changes.

Regularly called into conference on cases pertaining to following area: (1) Problems resulting from automation with job changes and force reduction. (2) Industrial relations and personnel policy as well as interpretation of policy. (3) Special training programs, personnel surveys.

Miscellaneous activities include:

1. Special assignments for Division Superintendent in matters relating to personnel and industrial relations policy, general budgets and costs, special programs, administration, etc.

2. Coordination and consultation on personnel matters with Industrial Relations, Employee Benefits, Training, Wage and Salary Administration, and other plant divisions.

3. Coordination of all division training programs; assignment of personnel to these programs.

4. Counselling on company benefits accruing to division personnel.

5. Supervision of special presentations and programs for company visitors and trainees.

6. Coordination of Division Emergency Service organization.

Reason for desiring change:

Upward move.

REFERENCES

Available

Synopsis of Resume of: 303 Lawton Rd.
SARAH RYAN   Orlando, FL 32803
                                                            Phone: (305) 423-5316

JOB OBJECTIVE

Legal Assistant (Paralegal); position in private law firm.

EMPLOYMENT

1978–Present   PUBLIC DEFENDER, Orlando, Florida.
Investigator.

1970–1978   SELF-EMPLOYED, Bradenton, Florida.
Owned and managed 75 rental-unit complex.

1965–1970   FARMERS BANK OF STATE OF DELAWARE, Georgetown,
Delaware.
Supervisor of Mortgage Loan Dept. Moved from area.

1958–1965   ALL AMERICAN ENGINEERING CO., Wilmington, Delaware.
Assistant to Technical Editor.

EDUCATION

1977–1978   Manatee Junior College, Bradenton, Florida (attended nights).
Associate of Science Degree in Legal Assistant Program. 72 hours.

Courses included:

Accounting, Economics, Written Communications, Government,
Human Relations, Law Office Mgmt. & Procedures, Legal
Terminology, Research, Real Property Law, Wills, Trusts & Probate,
Principles of Family Law, Civil & Criminal Procedures, General
Law, Intro to Litigation and Evidence, Criminal Law.

PERSONAL

Born: 1/2/41; single; health - excellent; owns home and car.
Hobbies: Spectator sports; sailing; reading.
Affiliations: Member National Association of Legal Assistants, Inc.
Member Orlando Sailing Club.

(FOR AMPLIFICATION PLEASE SEE FOLLOWING)
Determined woman who decided to change fields in her late thirties and pursue a lifelong interest in law.
"Talked herself" into a good job in this comparatively new field. Resume focus strictly on legal aspect.

Amplified Resume   Sarah Ryan - page 2

LEGAL EMPLOYMENT HIGHLIGHTS

1978–Present

After receiving Associate Degree as Legal Assistant, approached Public Defender requesting permission to work as intern for a three month period at no salary in order to gain additional, practical, on-the-job experience and training. Request reluctantly granted.

Applied herself diligently and at conclusion of trial period was offered and accepted full-time position of "Investigator."

In this capacity, primary function is handling Juvenile and Misdemeanor investigations, as well as overflow of felony cases.

Interviews incarcerated defendants and assists them in obtaining reasonable bonds. Interviews persons being held in Juvenile Detention for daily hearings.

Assists "walk-ins" needing help and advice on a court proceeding as well as general information pertaining to the processes involved in obtaining a public defender (prior to arraignment).

Does follow-up work relative to interviews; interviews witnesses, arranges for photographs, makes all diagrams and tabulates any related evidence for use in ultimate defense. Evaluates, coordinates all evidence and information which is discussed with attorneys.

Maintains good public relations with all other governmental agencies involved in the Criminal Justice System, as well as the lawyers and co-workers in Public Defender's employ.

Attends sundry seminars to keep abreast of new methods, procedures and general updating to aid and improve job performance.

Reason for desiring change: Thoroughly enjoys work and responsibilities; would make change only to private law firm with greater remuneration and less pressure.

REFERENCES

Available. Please no present employer contact at this time.

Synopsis of Resume of:
ROBERT E. SANDERSON

69 Canterbury Rd.
Corning, NY 14820
Phone: (716) 897–4676

JOB OBJECTIVE

Position in field of Marketing or Sales Supervision.

EMPLOYMENT

1978–6/80	**EASTERN SALES MANAGER** Boyden Equipment Co., 80 Broad St., Chicago, IL
2/74–11/77	**ASSISTANT TO GENERAL SALES MANAGER** (Moved up from trainee - through Sales Staff Group) Scovell-Hill Inc., Schenectady, NY
1971–1974	**ASSISTANT TO PRESIDENT**, various firms: Morgan Machine Tool Co., Universal Sports Car Sales, Foley Farm Equipment Co., Rochester, NY
1964–1969	**OWNER-MGR.** (liquidated on service recall) Sanderson Appliance Co., Buffalo, NY

EDUCATION

1959–1962	Niagara University, Niagara, NY B.S. in M.E. Offered fellowship; declined to enter service.
Other:	University of Buffalo Course in "Chemistry." Evening School. U.S. Navy courses in: Industrial Mgmt., Strategy and Tactics, Logistics.

SERVICE

1962–1964	U.S. Navy. Completed N.R.O.T.C. in college. Currently holds rank of Commander in Reserve; is not required to participate in active duty.

PERSONAL

Born:	6/18/41 in Buffalo, NY. Height 5'10"; wt. 172 lbs.
Married:	Wife graduate Syracuse University; 2 children, ages: 14, 12.
Residence:	Owns home; willing to relocate for proper opportunity.
Affiliations:	Toastmasters' Club; Rotary; active in politics.

(FOR AMPLIFICATION PLEASE SEE FOLLOWING)
*Classic responsibility-result record, reflecting able man quickly taking situation in hand, assuming
additional responsibilities, with corresponding accomplishment.*

Amplified Resume   Robert E. Sanderson

EMPLOYMENT HIGHLIGHTS

1978–6/80
BOYDEN EQUIPMENT COMPANY
(Mfr's bulk milk cooling equipment)

Employed to direct company's sales effort in an area encompassing: New York State, Vermont, Conn., New Hampshire, and Maine. In Canada: Ontario, Quebec and the Maritime Provinces.

Equipment is sold for use on individual dairy farms to store and cool milk prior to its collection. Sales are channeled through direct salesmen, manufacturers' representatives, distributors, dealers and direct major accounts. These include Agway, United Cooperatives of Quebec, and other cooperatives or marketing groups who buy for members. Competition is intense, with over 50 competitive firms in area.

Hires, trains, fires, directs salesmen; makes territorial changes. Selects distributors and dealers, recommends credit limit for final decision by Credit Department. Works with dealer and distributor personnel, as well as direct salesmen, to aid and stimulate sales effort.

Results

1) Tripled an original dollar sales volume of low 6 figures.
2) Increased major direct cooperative accts. from 4 to 10.
3) Added 9 key area distributors, plus 7 key dealers.
4) Achieved effective distribution in all Canadian areas.
5) Company valuation of services indicated by an increase of $5,000 on a substantial starting yearly income.

Reason for change: Employed with understanding would become General Manager of company within short period. Recent change in company ownership makes appointment and/or further progress with company unlikely. Resigned.

2/74–11/77
SCOVELL-HILL INC.
(Mfr's glassed steel and alloy equipment)
Yearly volume: $50 million

Employed as trainee; moved into Sales Staff Group. Activities included the following:

(continued)

Amplified Resume   Robert Sanderson

SCOVELL-HILL INC. employment continued

(1) Established, organized and directed a market research and analysis group.
(2) Prepared annual sales budget for management approval.
(3) Developed sales training program for field sales engineers.
(4) Developed refresher training and product information programs for established field sales group.

Appointed Assistant to General Sales Mgr. Interviewed, recommended personnel for Sales Division. Established sales territories for field force of 40; established territorial and individual quotas.

Designated by company's Executive V. President to set up and conduct technical seminars for executive and supervisory customer personnel. Similar seminars had been conducted for several years; however, improved handling resulted in expanded interest and brought increased opportunity to acquaint participants with company products. In addition, sales increase resulted, with one sale of over $1 million directly on specifications conceived at one meeting.

Became interested in a line of milk coolers produced by Scovell-Hill; envisioned immense market potential; assumed responsibility for promotion. Created a distribution system in face of established competition; sales increased steadily.

Reason for change: Received promising offer from Boyden. Higher salary, General Manager potential in near future. Resigned to accept.

PRIOR

Formed Sanderson Appliance Co.; built it to yearly volume of $500,000 with 8 salesmen and 10 servicemen. Added sales of commercial refrigeration and heavy air conditioning equipment. Achieved solid profit.

Recalled to Naval Service with 90 day grace period. Liquidated business. Upon reporting to active duty, was advised emergency passed, services would not be required.

Having liquidated own business, accepted employment as Assistant to President of various firms, on temporary consulting basis. Offered permanent post with Scovell-Hill Inc. Accepted.

REFERENCES

Available

Synopsis of Resume of:
RACHEL R. PRINCE

879 Big Pass Rd.
Sarasota, FL 33581
Phone: (813) 349–9887

CAREER OBJECTIVE

Assistant to executive, preferably in field of arts. Completely unencumbered, free to travel and work any necessary overtime, including holidays.

CAREER EXPERIENCE

1979–Present	MARIE SELBY BOTANICAL GARDENS, Sarasota, Florida. Public Relations - Editor of Bulletin.
1978–1979	FLORIDA WEST COAST SYMPHONY, Sarasota, Florida. General Manager.
1976–1978	CASEY KEY OBSERVER, Sarasota, Florida. Weekly newspaper. Production Manager for newspaper with 20,000 circulation.
1969–1976	AREA HIGH SCHOOLS. Math tutor.
Misc:	FREE-LANCE. Public relations for community theatre groups.

EDUCATION

College:	Vassar College, Poughkeepsie, N.Y. Major: Math. Minors: Art and German.
Other:	Courses in Commercial Art and Shorthand.
Skills:	Fluent German. Typewriter, dictaphone typesetters (Compugraphic and IBM composer) headliner machines.
Travel:	Lived in Germany, Philippines, China, Japan, Hawaii, as daughter and wife of army officers. On own as widow has traveled to: England, Greece, Brazil.

PERSONAL

Born:	1925; health - excellent; no physical limitations.
Marital status:	Widow; two grown, self-supporting daughters.
Finances:	Good order - owns home and car.
Hobbies:	Swimming (Red Cross Water Safety Instructor); sailing.
Affiliations:	Ringling Museum; Girl Scouts; Asolo Opera Society.

(FOR AMPLIFICATION SEE FOLLOWING)

Unencumbered widow with multiple skills desires to put them to use in general assistant capacity. Dislikes 9-to-5-type job; loves travel. Consequently complete freedom to do so emphasized, along with willingness to work odd, any and all hours or days.

Amplified Resume   Rachel R. Prince

CAREER HIGHLIGHTS

1979–Present
MARIE SELBY BOTANICAL GARDENS

In public relations area, coordinates fund raising functions, including the garden weddings which number in excess of 40 each year. As Editor of Bulletin, responsible for selection of all materials to be included in the bi-monthly publication. Edits, typesets, and lays out bulletin pages. Writes some material for publication and all news releases. Fills in for Communications Director in his absence.

1978–1979
FLORIDA WEST COAST SYMPHONY

As General Manager, responsible for all business aspects of the full symphony orchestra: budgeting, staff supervision, volunteers, contract negotiations with artist/soloist agents, musical contracts, grant applications. Wrote and disseminated publicity and public relations material.

1976–1978
CASEY KEY OBSERVER

Full responsibility for entire layout and paste-up of tabloid size paper. Did portions of same on part-time basis during daughters' dependent years.

1969–1976
MATHEMATICS TUTORING

Substitute mathematics teacher at various area schools, as well as private home tutoring.

PRIOR AND OVERSEAS

General office work for Secretary of the Air Force and his aide, statistical analyst for Hawaiian Economic Foundation. Both positions required degree of travel. Excellent letters of recommendation as to caliber of work and efficiency of travel arrangements.

GENERAL

Passport current.

REFERENCES

On Request.

Resume of:
PAUL H. CARPENTER

149 Palmer Ave.
Des Moines, IA 50315
Phone: (515) 631–0551

JOB OBJECTIVE

Position as Insurance Specialist (Casualty, Fire, Marine) for bank or banking real estate dept., or position where extensive management experience can be fully utilized.

EMPLOYMENT

1962–6/80
MANAGER
Des Moines Casualty Insurance Co.

Employed as Underwriter. Approved or rejected business written for all forms of casualty insurance. Required expert knowledge of property evaluation, ability to judge past performance of individuals, and justify decision to salesman and property owner if rejected. In 4 years promoted to Assistant Manager. In 1971 promoted to Manager. Duties similar with more responsibility inherent in Manager's spot.

Directed approximately 35 full time employees; supervised efforts of 125 agents. Continuously recruited, encouraged, trained and worked with new personnel. Worked with agents through approximately 6 special agents in the office; was final authority on problems wiich persisted. Hired and trained office, clerical, and accounting personnel. Supervised prompt processing of applications and policies, collection of delinquencies, and handled claims from insureds.

During term as Manager, company went through reorganization and top management change. Company policy dictated drastic cutbacks and economies in all offices, plus a change in representation policies. As a direct result of the latter, Des Moines office lost agencies, taking with them a substantial six figure volume in premiums.

RECORD DURING MANAGEMENT PERIOD

More than regained loss above; has increased dollar volume. Properly and promptly handled and processed the increased volume, plus paper work resulting from agency changes, with force of 15 compared with over 30 to start. Expanded full company services to the large area surrounding Des Moines, whereas only fire had been offered previously outside Polk County.

Reason for resignation: Impending transfer to undesirable location.

(continued)

Synopsis page avoided in record of older man where last or present employment has been of considerable duration. Immediate employment amplification serves to put immediate focus on most significant aspect of record—namely, experience.

EMPLOYMENT
continued

1952–1962
PARTNER
Empire Insurers Agency, Des Moines, IA

With partner formed company. Acted as underwriter and office mgr. Provided better than average livelihood during difficult depression and war years. Company dissolved when partner was forced to withdraw for reasons of health.

1940–1952
UNDERWRITER
Bismarck Casualty & Surety Co., Bismarck, ND

Employed as office boy and clerk. Promoted to underwriter; put through extensive training and self training program before competent to act on own responsibility.

1946 transferred to Des Moines, Iowa, with larger responsibility. Record was such invited by superior to join him in forming above company. Resigned to do so.

EDUCATION

High school graduate; Underwriters Board courses in various phases of insurance; numerous company courses in casualty, marine and general insurance.

PERSONAL

Born:	6/17/21 in Davenport, IA. Height 5'8"; wt. 170 lbs.
Married:	5 children, 4 no longer dependent.
Health:	Good; no physical limitations; last physical 6/79.
Finances:	Excellent; no debt encumbrance.
Residence:	Owns home; will relocate for exceptional opportunity.
Affiliations:	Rotary Club; Chamber of Commerce.

REFERENCES

Available on request.

Synopsis of Resume of:
ROSEMARY LONDON

998 Chapel St.
New Haven, CT 06510
Phone: (203) 927–5771

JOB OBJECTIVE

Position as Medical Assistant, 30–35 hrs. per week, perferably with regular hours and schedule important for diabetic management.

EDUCATION

1980   Whittier Vocational School, New Haven, Conn.
      Medical Assistant Program encompassing:
Administrative
      Scheduling and receiving patients; obtaining patients' data; maintaining medical records; typing and medical transcription; handling phones and correspondence; office care, management, insurance matters, accounts, collection.
Clinical
      Preparing patient for examination; obtaining vital signs; taking medical histories; assisting with treatments; performing routine office lab procedures and electrocardiograms; sterilizing instruments and equipment; instructing patients in preparation for x-ray and tests.

Other: Community College, Glenside, Pennsylvania
      Business courses.

Special Skills
Typing, medical transcribing Peg Board, routine bookkeeping, billing, collections, interviewing, CPR, EKG, Aseptic Technique, Venipuncture, Finger Stick, Injections, Basic Laboratory.

Special Knowledge
Diabetes Mellitus and Insulin. Lectured in field for Medical Assistant Program. Invited back as guest lecturer for future classes. Circumstances permitting, desires to become active in instruction of diabetics as part of, or in addition to, medical assistant duties.

Certification
National Certification Examination. American Association of Medical Assistants.

PERSONAL

Born 1932; health - excellent, Diabetes Mellitus, Class I. Single, one self-supporting son; owns home, car; will travel and relocate.

EMPLOYMENT

1951–1970   PRODUCTION SUPERVISOR promoted from contract analyst.
      Conn. General Life Insurance Co., Hartford, Conn.
      5 yr. marriage hiatus. See amplification.

(Example of physical problem which must be acknowledged but not dwelled upon, with emphasis on current and transferrable skills in new field).

Amplified Resume   Rosemary London

EMPLOYMENT HIGHLIGHTS

1951–1960
CONNECTICUT GENERAL LIFE INSURANCE CO.

Employed initially as group insurance contract analyst. Promoted to Production Supervisor, Group Insurance Underwriting which encompassed training and lecturing as well as setting up and conducting workshops. Left for marriage.

1965–1970

Returned after divorce in less demanding job as assistant to personnel manager. Screened and interviewed job applicants; took dictation as well as handling correspondence on own; supervised payroll. Left to spend more time with young son.

1970–1980
COMMUNITY INVOLVEMENT

As member of League of Women's Voters, used writing, research and editorial skills for brochures and press releases. Also lectured and assisted in formation of speakers' bureau.

Named Concert Chairman of Community Concert Association, was responsible for all local arrangements for visiting artists (transportation and accommodations), staging and union liaison.

Researched dietetic nutrition, organized support group for exchange of information.

GENERAL

With son no longer dependent, desires to enter new field, fully utilizing former solid experience and newly acquired education and skills. Member American Association of Medical Assistants, and American Diabetes Association.

REFERENCES

On Request

Synopsis of Resume of:
ALLAN S. FOGEL

27 Whitney Rd.
Chagrin Falls, OH 44022
Phone: (216) 897–3210

OBJECTIVE

Supervisor or Asst. Supervisor in the Mortgage Lending Field.

EMPLOYMENT

8/77–Present	Secretary - Mortgage & Real Estate Department. First National Bank, Cleveland, OH
1973–1977	Manager Electric Supply Div. Mohawk Electric, Columbus, OH (Yearly salary increased by $5,850 during tenure).
1962–1973	Field Investigator. Credit Men's Association, Battle Creek, MI
Prior	Part-time work for electrical contractor.

EDUCATION

1958–1962	Ohio State University. B.S. in Business Administration. Dean's List 4 semesters.
Other:	Credit Management Course. Real Estate Course.

PERSONAL

Born:	3/18/40 in Cleveland, OH. Height 5′9″; wt. 175 lbs.
Married:	2 children, ages 11 and 9.
Health:	Excellent; no physical limitations; last physical 1979.
Residence:	Rents; free to relocate for proper opportunity.
Hobbies:	Numismatics; Chess; Skeet.
Affiliations:	Ohio State Alumni Association (past President); Cleveland Builders Association; Rotary International.

(FOR AMPLIFICATION SEE FOLLOWING)
Stressing success achieved in diversified fields, all contributing to overall qualifications for more responsible post in highly specialized field.

Amplified Resume   Page 2

EMPLOYMENT HIGHLIGHTS

8/77–Present
FIRST NATIONAL BANK

Upon completion of bank's training program, was put in charge of operations of New Business Department. Supervised development of an officer-calling program to encourage new business; personally made over 200 calls on established and prospective customers. Helped develop the offering of automated services for customers and prospects. These included payroll processing. Was elected Secretary of company during this period.

April 1979 was given added title of Assistant Mortgage Officer. Responsibilities included originating residential and commercial mortgages plus construction loans. Efforts continue to be concentrated in this area. Supervises 16 personnel.

Results:

(1) Mortgage portfolio has increased from $42 million to $49 million.

(2) Made significant contact with secondary mortgage market as initial step in relieving bank of poor yield, long term mortgages.

(3) Acknowledged as driving force in stimulating action in mortgage area which has resulted in steadily increasing volume.

Reason for desiring change: Increased income.

1973–1979
MOHAWK ELECTRIC

Initially employed as Assistant Credit Manager for 6-county division doing sales volume in 8 figures. Supervised credit extension, collections and routine details.

Results:

(1) Brought credit situation into proper balance, with accounts up-to-date or in a collection procedure.

1975 promoted to Credit Manager with same general responsibilities but added authority. In 6 months promoted again to Operating Manager with increased salary and responsibilities. They included: (1) Procurement, (2) Credit, (3) Office Management, (4) Personnel management and evaluation.

(continued)

Amplified Resume   Page 3

MOHAWK ELECTRIC employment continued:

During his tenure volume of sales increased substantially, while being handled by 6 less personnel; operation was below budget estimates each year; personnel turnover minimal.

Reason for leaving: To accept better position.

1962–1973
CREDIT MEN'S ASSOCIATION

Upon graduation from college, was employed as credit checker while taking Credit Mgmt. Course.

Upon completion of course, promoted steadily to supervision of Field Investigators who worked on a case fee basis.

Indication of employer satisfaction of efforts shown by steady increase in salary and responsibilities, as well as being kept on salary for approximately one year while recuperating from injuries suffered in automobile accident which occurred during employment.

Reason for leaving: To improve status.

REFERENCES

On Request

Synopsis of Resume of:
MARTHA HARVEY

987 West Ave.
Detroit, MI 48224
Phone: (313) 993–8754

JOB OBJECTIVE

Director of Nurses

EXPERIENCE

1974–1980	Supervisor of 15 operating rooms. Miami Valley Hospital School of Nursing Dayton, OH
1967–1970	Director of Nursing Service Staten Island Memorial Hospital
1963–1965	Operating Room Nurse St. Mary's Hospital, Rock Island, IL

EDUCATION

B.S. in Nursing, Keuka College, NY.

R.N. - Strong Memorial Hospital, Rochester, NY

Other: Extension courses from University of Southern California School of
Medicine.

Current: Courses in Psychiatry

PERSONAL

Born: 1941; Baltimore, MD. Widow.
Health: Good; height 5'5"; wt. 140.
Finances: Good order; no dependents.
Hobbies: Community involvement.

(FOR AMPLIFICATION PLEASE SEE FOLLOWING)
*Mature woman who has resumed career in nursing and wants administration. Glowing letters of
recommendation tell the story so well, excerpts are effectively used.*

Amplified Resume   Martha Harvey

EXPERIENCE

1974–1980

Resumed career upon death of husband; accepted position as supervisor of hospital's 15 operating rooms. Was assured of promotion to Director of Nursing Service which has not materialized due to factors which will be discussed at interview.

Would make change anywhere within continental United States for position in administration.

1967–1970

Employed as operating room supervisor, in two years was named Director of Nursing. Excerpts from letters of recommendation during her tenure read in part "...Mrs. Harvey built a nursing staff unequalled anywhere. She has great foresight, many ideas and high moral character with the ability to transmit all of this to persons who work for her."

Relative to her innovations and accomplishments: "...She developed the cardiac nursing station where there was a higher nurse-patient ratio than anywhere else...she helped organize the LPN training programs at vocational schools...her dedication has contributed immeasureably to the growth of medicine and health care in the community."

Reason for leaving:

Retired upon marriage.

1963–1965

Employed as operating room nurse; in approximately one year promoted to supervisor. On own time assisted director of nurses, who recommended she return to college for degree to become scholastically qualified for administration. Did so.

REFERENCES

On Request

Synopsis of Resume of:
RUTH ROGERS

862 Rupert St.
McLean, VA 22101
Phone: (202) 632–9844

OBJECTIVE

General Duty Nursing

EXPERIENCE

1976–Present   Millville Veterans Hospital, Falls Church, VA
'76–'78 - General Duty - Amputee Ward.
'78–   Charge Nurse - Paraplegic Ward.

1974–1976   Caldwell County Hospital, Alexandria, VA
'74–'75 - Emergency Room Supervisor
'75–'76 - Surgical Head Nurse

1968–1974   Mercy Hospital, Hornell, NY
St. Mary's Hospital, Rochester, NY
   General duty nursing

EDUCATION

1964–1966   University of Michigan
   Liberal Arts

1966–1968   Hospital School of Nursing, Kalamazoo, MI
   R.N. Degree

Other: State Board Examination:
   California, New York, Virginia

Current: Courses in Geriatrics, Cardiac, Shock

Affiliations: American Nurses Association
Michigan State Nurse Association
University Hospital Nurses Alumni Ass'n.

PERSONAL

Born: 1938 in Hopkins, MN. Widow; one minor dependent.
Health: Excellent; no physical limitations; height 5'7"; wt. 135.
Hobbies: Bridge; theater; tennis; golf.
Misc.   Have necessary clearance required for dispensing drugs.

(FOR AMPLIFICATION PLEASE SEE FOLLOWING)
An average record polished to appear brighter through emphasis on ability to cope with change, and scrupulously follow orders.

Amplified Resume   Ruth Rogers

EXPERIENCE

1976–Present
Millville Veterans Hospital, Falls Church, CA

Accepted position in Amputee Ward after becoming familiar with the facility due to terminal illness of veteran husband. In 1978, promoted to Charge Nurse in the Paraplegic Ward. Supervised all professional personnel assigned to the unit, including those in the physical therapy area. Have found work satisfying and gratifying; have established excellent relations with patients, subordinates and superiors; have been offered opportunity to raise present classification.

Reason for desiring change: Death of husband and desire to affiliate with non-government facility.

1974–1976
Caldwell County Hospital, Alexandria, VA

After marriage relocated in Virginia and accepted temporary position as staff nurse. In four months was offered, and accepted, position as Emergency Room Supervisor. Filled in occasionally as Surgical Head Nurse, and when vacancy occurred was offered permanent position in that capacity.

Reason for leaving: Terminal illness of husband.

1968–1974
Mercy Hospital, St. Mary's Hospital, Hornell & Rochester, NY

As general duty staff nurse, supervised professional and non-professional workers assigned to work area; relieved Charge Nurse when required. In general, made preliminary observations of patients' conditions; prepared them for medical treatment. Took histories, kept charts, assisted physicians with physical examinations and treatments. In addition, prepared equipment for treatment and tests; instructed patients in home care. Observed symptoms; noted case progress as well as results of medical and nursing treatment. Attended personal needs of patients; administered special diets, medicines and treatment as prescribed. Assisted physicians with treatments, dressings and examination preparation. Kept records of narcotics and other drugs signed out; received special recognition for detecting irregularities in records.

Reason for leaving: To get married.

GENERAL: Excellent references from employers available on request.

Synopsis of Resume of:
ALMA D. LOGAN

498 Walnut St.
Canton, OH 44702
Phone: (216) 654-3033

JOB OBJECTIVE

Private duty Licensed Practical Nursing

CHRONOLOGY

1980-Present	Private duty LPN work through church references. Part-time private duty cases through Morgan Health Services.
1979-1980	Canton School of Practical Nursing. Graduated as LPN.
1977-1979	Operated baby sitting service from own home; also moved in to care for children while parents on vacation.
1973-1977	Secretary to Director of Personnel, University of Conn. Health Center. Resigned to relocate in Canton, Ohio.
1946-1973	Legal Secretary, United Airlines Outside Sales Representative.

EDUCATION

1940-1946	Central High School, Bridgeport, Conn. Phyllis Bell School Modeling, Washington, D.C. Porter School of Business, Washington, D.C. Berlitz School of Languages, Washington, D.C.
1979-1980	Canton School of Practical Nursing. • Instruction included: Body Structure and Function, Vocational Adjustments, Life Span, Health, Nutrition, Obstetrics, Pediatrics, Medical-Surgical, Psychiatry, Geriatrics.
Languages:	Limited Spanish and French.

PERSONAL

Born:	1926; Height 5'5"; wt. 115; divorced, no children.
Health:	Excellent. Owns car; rents; free to relocate.
Hobbies:	Bicycling; working with children; yoga; golf; swimming.
Affiliations:	Member "Sweet Adelines" Barbershop Singing group. Member LPN Association of Ohio.

(FOR AMPLIFICATION PLEASE SEE FOLLOWING)

*Survivor who has made complete change of field. Confused background cleared up through "chronology"
technique as well as the dateless groupings on page 2, slanted to point up responsible qualities important
in present (new) field.*

Amplified Resume   Alma Logan - page 2

EMPLOYMENT HIGHLIGHTS

University of Conn. Health Center

In addition to standard duties as secretary to Director of Personnel, was V.P. of Health Center Association's Hospital Auxiliary. Headed up United Way Appeal for 2,000 employees.

Prepared correspondence for employer's signature; set up conferences, meetings; prepared grant forms. Handled office unassisted while employer on 3-month sabbatical.

Upon resignation to relocate, given excellent letter of reference from employer reading in part: "Optimistic, cheerful, possesses high stability. Gets along well with others, has a high tolerance of people, faith in social institutions and understanding of other people and their human weaknesses."

Legal Secretary

Screened jury lists, prepared court calendars, handled general correspondence, as well as general secretarial work.

Sales Representative

Acted as outside sales representative contacting travel agents in New York City, Washington, D. C., Richmond, Baltimore, Philadelphia, and Norfolk. Also worked as ticket counter agent.

Miscellaneous

Did volunteer missionary work in summer of 1978, in Republic of Panama through church. Lived at an orphanage for a month with 35 Spanish-speaking girls.

Presently volunteer youth advisor for teenagers who meet Sunday evenings at Episcopal Church.

REFERENCES

Letters of reference and rating reports available upon request.

Synopsis of Resume of:
WARNER WALKER

553 Couch St.
Portland, OR 97209
Phone: (503) 229–9050

JOB OBJECTIVE

Position in two to three doctor office, utilizing paramedic training and experience.

EXPERIENCE

1977–Present	SOUTH COUNTY FIRE DEPARTMENT, Portland, Oregon. Journeyman Fire Fighter/Paramedic.
1971–1977	LANTERN ELECTRIC CO., Portland, Oregon, Estimator-bidder - promoted from electrician's helper.
1970–1971	RAYBRO ELECTRIC CO., Baker, Oregon From stock boy to front office.
1968–1970	Interim jobs while recuperating from leg wound sustained during Marine Corps duty in Vietnam.

SERVICE

1966–1968	Marine Corps; trained at Paris Island; Vietnam duty. Purple Heart; Good Conduct Medal; Hon. Discharge.

EDUCATION

1966	Baker High School, Baker, Oregon. Graduated.
Other:	Marine Corp. courses in radio repair. Emergency Medical Tech. Course I - 200 hours. Emergency Medical Tech. Course II - 500 hours.

LICENSES

Fixed Wing and Helicopter pilot's license.

PERSONAL

Age: 32	Born 5/30/48. Married, 2 children, height 6'; wt. 160.
Health:	Excellent. Owns home, car, willing to relocate.
Hobbies:	Flying; scuba diving; snow skiing; chess.
Affiliations:	State Fire Fighters Assoc.

(FOR AMPLIFICATION PLEASE SEE FOLLOWING)

Comparatively new field open to both men and women. Thrust of resume is on this young man's hard-core experience in the paramedic field, as well as temperament—important in a field requiring cool head in emergency.

Amplified Resume   Warner Walker - page 2

PARAMEDIC EXPERIENCE

1977–Present
SOUTH COUNTY FIRE DEPARTMENT (Combined Fire and Ambulance Rescue Service)

Accepted in department after careful screening and background check as to morals, temperament, ability to live in close quarters, physical stamina, emotional stability and genuine concern for people.

Completed necessary courses for state certification in fire fighting; promoted through ranks to present status of Journeyman Fire Fighter.

Due to unique operation combining fire and ambulance services, firemen are encouraged to take free medical technician training made available at local vocational school and hospitals.

Took and passed the Emergency Medical Technician's Course I which stresses: emergency care, maintenance of airway, control of bleeding, shock management, emergency baby delivery and basic life support.

Continued through EMT–II to become fully qualified Paramedic. At this level "scene evaluation" is added, along with cardio-pulmonary resuscitation, intubation, defibrilation, IV's and drugs, as well as advanced life support.

As a Paramedic is permitted to work on own responsibility following strict protocol, through IV's to defibrilation if warranted. Calls hospital, acts as "doctor's long arm", meticulously following physician's verbal phone instructions until patient's removal to the hospital.

Works 24 hr. shift, followed by 48 hr. off-duty. During duty hours teaches basic first aid to fire fighter apprentices, in addition to standard fire fighting duties and ambulance response.

Reason for desiring change: Although twice cited for fire fighting action, feels that, by temperament, is better suited to paramedic aspect of job in which he excells. Would prefer position with small staff of private doctors who could utilize his training and practical know-how in their work.

REFERENCES

On Request

Resume of JACK J. JOHNSON

4004 Poplar St.
Memphis, TN 38104
Phone: (901) 794–7976

JOB OBJECTIVE

Part-time work afternoons and week-ends while attending school mornings. Experienced in construction, dry-wall finishing, bartending, short-order cook.

EXPERIENCE

1975–1976   Self-employed as dry-wall finisher following service '74–'75. Discontinued due to building moratorium, and decision to continue education.

1976–1978   Employed as short-order cook weekends while attending college days. Second job as private bartender on call by local caterer for evenings. Resigned both jobs for better paying part-time job next below.

1979–1980   MacElwain Construction Co., Memphis, Tenn. Flagman, general construction and handyman. Hours proved incompatible with present school requirements. Resigned with re-hire status.

Misc: Worked every summer during high school at miscellaneous jobs including: McDonalds, drive-in theatre snack bar.

EDUCATION

1970–1974   Chattanooga High School. Graduated.

1976–Pres.   Community College, Memphis, Tenn.
             Medical Laboratory Technician Program scheduled for completion 1981. Ultimate goal: Medical Technologist Research.

PERSONAL

Born: 11/11/53. Single. Height 5'11". Weight 166 lbs.
Health: Excellent. Resides with parents; owns car.
Hobbies: Astronomy; songwriting; reading; science.
Service: U.S. Air Force. Radio Communications specialist. Hon. Discharge.

REFERENCES AVAILABLE FROM ALL FORMER EMPLOYERS
Synopsis deleted in favor of chronology format aiding glance-clear analysis of young man's part-time work history. Emphasis on reliability and satisfaction given in part-time employments as such jobs are plagued with "no-shows", and a general casual acceptance of responsibility.

Synopsis of Resume of:
ALAN L. THOMASON

30 Sutton St.
Hattiesburg, MS 39401
Phone: (601) 761–4132

JOB OBJECTIVE

Position in field of Personnel, College Recruitment, or College Relations.

EMPLOYMENT

10/77–Present   DIRECTOR OF PLACEMENT & ALUMNI RELATIONS
ASSISTANT DIRECTOR OF ADMISSIONS
Miss. Southern College, Hattiesburg, MS

1976–1977   PURCHASING AGENT (resigned to accept better position above)
Randolph Chemical Co., Butler, AL

1966–1976   Summers and part time during college years:
Red Cross Swimming Instructor.

EDUCATION

1966–1970   Allendale Preparatory School, Lake Charles, LA
Valedictorian of class; awarded year's scholarship for European
study and travel

1973–1976   University of Arkansas
Degree: B.S. in Social Sciences.
Standing: 48 in class of 55. Dean's List 4 times.
Expenses: Earned approximately 75%.
Activities: President of: Junior and Senior class,
Student Board of Governors, Inter-
College Council of American Red Cross.
Member of: Glee Club, Debating Team.

PERSONAL

Born: 3/15/53 in Butler, AL. Height 5'10"; wt. 175. Married, no children.
Residence: College quarters; free to relocate.
Hobbies: Swimming; sailing, stamp collecting.
Affiliations: Southern College Personnel Officers Association; Miss. State Deans
& Guidance Counselors Ass'n.; Miss. State Counselors Association.

(FOR AMPLIFICATION SEE FOLLOWING)
*Although shooting for industry, stress put on extraordinary accomplishments in present position,
demonstrating the energy and initiative obviously usable and desirable in any field.*

Amplified Resume   Alan L. Thomason

EMPLOYMENT HIGHLIGHTS

10/77–Present
MISS. SOUTHERN COLLEGE

Originally employed as Assistant Director of Placement and Admissions. Promoted to present classification after one year.

As Director of Placement is responsible for senior and alumni placement, plus teacher placement and part time and summer positions for under-graduates. In addition, does student advising and counseling, with job and ability evaluation.

As Assistant Director of Admissions, has set up a system of recruitment for the college. Gives talks before high school students and various other youth groups in the 15 county area, arousing and stimulating interest in Mississippi Southern College. Later, passes on qualifications of those who apply.

In placement field has made extensive contact with desirable companies; has built companies interviewing students from 75 to 120. Furthers this interest by speaking before various civic organizations. Keeps posted on requirements for a variety of fields and positions, then steers interviewers to right prospects. Entire program has been highly successful; relations with students and industry, excellent.

In newly created position of Director of Alumni Relations inaugurated a policy of regular contact; serves as liaison between alumni, faculty, and students.

Results have been positive.

1. Dues paying alumni percentage raised from 11% to 39%. (National average is approximately 19%).

2. Participation in insurance program benefiting college raised from 20% to 35%.

3. Initiated a systematic contribution program supplementing the above.

General:

1) Serves as Chariman of Committee on Scholarship. As members are Deans, PHD's, and persons of similar stature, unusual tact is required.

2) Coordinates Graduate School studies; advises on financial aid available.

Reason for desiring change: Greater income.

REFERENCES

Available

Synopsis of Resume of:
KEITH M. KNIGHT

670 James St.
Madison, WI 53705
Phone: (608) 227–9882

JOB OBJECTIVE

Position in field of Photography: Journalistic, Illustrative,
(industrial, documentary, publicity).

EDUCATION

1975–1979	Dubuque University, Dubuque, IA
	Graduated 6/79. Bachelor of Fine Arts Degree.
	Major: Photographic Illustration. Minor: Photo Journalism.
	Expenses: Earned all over G.I. Bill. Standing: upper third.
	Activities: member Camera Club and Photographic Society.
1973	Deveaux Art Institute (Correspondence)
	Commercial Art.
1969–1971	Lawrence Vocational Institute, Madison, WI
	Engineering Math., Machine Design.

EMPLOYMENT

Following summer employments in Madison, WI:

1978	Hayden C. Holden (Commercial Photographer)
	All phases color lab. - dye transfer.
1977	Carhart Photo Finishing
	Photofinishing. Distribution color materials for processing.
1976	Madison Recorder (weekly newspaper)
	Assistant to staff photographer.
1969–1972	Philan Co. (heavy equipment machine shop.)
	Part time cooperative plan with Lawrence Vocational Inst. from 1970–'72; full time until left for service.
	Drafting, welding drawings, design work.

PERSONAL

Born:	3/3/50 in Preston, MN. Height 6′ Weight 190.
Married:	Wife graduate Layton School of Art; no children.
Health:	Excellent; no physical limitations; last physical - 1979.
Residence:	Rents apartment; free to relocate.
Hobbies:	Travel; Hunting; Fishing.
Service:	USA 1973–75; please see amplification.

(FOR AMPLIFICATION SEE FOLLOWING)
Emphasis on education pertinent to field of endeavor; experience and achievements also pertinent.

Amplified Resume   Keith M. Knight

EDUCATION

Dubuque University.
Courses completed include the following:

Technical

Course	Hrs.	Course	Hrs.
Photo Chemistry	6	Photo Optics	4
Photo Physics	4	Art Trends	8
Photo Sensitometry	4	Visual Communication	15
Photo Color	24	Communication Techniques	8
Photo Journalism	6	General Chemistry	8
Photo Illustration	22	Basic Photography	22

Cultural & General

Course			
Effective Speaking	3	Human Relations Workshop	4
Law & Society	2	International Affairs	4
Logic	3	Social Problems	3
Literature	6	Man in the Natural World	4
Economics	4		
Civilization	8		

SERVICE RECORD

1973–1975
U.S. Army
Completed course in cartography; served in Europe as Cartographic Draftsman. Became interested in photography and was permitted to use darkroom in spare time. Took advantage of all available instruction on the subject; competed in several post photographic contests; won several, received honorable mention in all.

GENERAL

1) During college period participated in several community activities. Included were: publicity pictures for fund raising drives and sundry benefit performances, youth group photos for use in brochures (YMCA, Scouts, etc.).

2) Photos displayed at Kern Galleries in Dubuque, Iowa, were selected for display at the state exhibit in Des Moines.

REFERENCES

Available on Request. Samples of work
available for review at interview.

Synopsis of Resume of:
PHILIP C. CONWELL

12 Kaiser Ave.
Boise, ID 83702
Phone: (208) 820–3001

JOB OBJECTIVE

Plant Manager or Supervision leading to Management post.

EMPLOYMENT

1976–Present
GENERAL MANAGER
Greer Mfg. Co., Boise, ID
(Mfr's. food handling equipment).

1973–1976
PRODUCTION CONTROL EXPEDITER
Hadden Meter Company, Boise, ID. (1,000 employees)
Resigned to accept position offer from above company.

Prior
Summer employments during college period;
machine shop assistant, construction worker, etc.

EDUCATION

1962–1965
Cloverdale Military Academy, Denver, CO

1965–1968
Montana State University, Missoula, MT
    Degree: B.S. in Business Administration.
    Expenses: Earned all over G.I. Bill assistance.
    Activities: Intramural sports; band.

SERVICE

1968–1972
U.S. Navy. Aviation Cadet to Ensign. Served as Flight
Instructor and Aide to Commanding Officer.
Honorably Released. Not in Reserves.

PERSONAL

Born: 7/25/47 in Denver, CO. Height 5'7"; wt. 150 lbs. Single.
Health: Good; no physical limitations.
Residence: Rents apartment; free to relocate.
Hobbies: Hunting; fishing; golf.
Affiliations: Chamber of Commerce; church member; political club (past
president).

(FOR AMPLIFICATION PLEASE SEE FOLLOWING)
*Responsibilities of major employment classified to demonstrate ability to cope with wide range of problems
involved in small plant management. Major plant expediting (indicated by number of employees)
important to well-rounded plant experience. However, as details of such work would be familiar to
prospective employers in this field, they are omitted.*

Amplified Resume   Philip C. Conwell

EMPLOYMENT HIGHLIGHTS

1976–Present
GREER MFG. COMPANY

Employed originally as Assistant General Manager with responsibilities similar, but in secondary authority, to those as Gen. Mgr. following promotion in 1976.

Business is family-owned and specializes in such products as complete handling centers for potatoes, onions, etc. Centers consist of graders, washers, conveyors, etc. Some combinations reach 75 feet in length with single installations selling in substantial 5 figure sums. Other items are designed and produced to perform special operations. Plant fabrication includes steel and wood with complete shop facilities for both mediums.

As General Manager, has complete charge of plant and production. Hires, fires, and directs a continuing training program for new employees. Responsibilities extend beyond plant, and include:

(1) Sales
Acting through dealers, does considerable work assisting them by actual customer contact. Makes direct sales.

(2) Prospectus
Surveys problem to be solved; makes initial sketches, followed by actual design and layout. Develops cost of components and fabrication; purchases required materials or components.

(3) Supervision
Supervises construction, and designates crew to follow shipment and assembly in purchasers' plant. In the event of operating problems after installation, makes personal check to find and implement solution.

(4) Public Relations
Excellent relations with plant personnel; has won cooperation and maximum effort. Good customer relations, successfully overcoming problems resulting from lack of technical skills in customer personnel.

Results: Under his direction plant has achieved a yearly dollar volume in substantial 6 figures; consistently operated at a profit.

Reason for desiring change: Feels has reached highest possible level in family operated business; would change for broader opportunity.

REFERENCES AVAILABLE

Synopsis of Resume of:
ROBERTA J. READ

90 Briarcliff Dr.
Lowell, MA 01853
Phone: (617) 266–1989

JOB OBJECTIVE

Private secretary or general secretarial work in small office. Familiar with personnel work, most office machines (including teletype, IBM accounting, etc.); can prepare financial reports; has all stenographic skills.

EMPLOYMENT

1978–Present   Typist, bookkeeper, general office work.
     Kaufman Distributing Company (vending machine distributors)
     20 Mill St., Lowell, MA

1975–1978   Typist, multilith operator, general office work.
     Alderson and Werder (Certified Public Accountants)
     804 Center Place, Lowell, MA

1971–1975   Personnel clerk, secretary
     Murray Personnel Service (employment agency)
     Hartford, CN

1968–1971   Stenographer
     Bruce & Allen (insurance agency)
     Hartford, CN

EDUCATION

High School: St. Ann's Academy, Norwalk, CN
     Graduated 1965.
College: Quinnipiac College, Hamden, CN
     Two-year secretarial course. 1965–1967.
General: Moderate knowledge of French and Spanish.

PERSONAL

Born: 10/13/47 in Norwalk, CN. Marital status: single.
Appearance: Height 5'2"; weight 110 lbs.
Health: Excellent; no physical limitations.
Residence: Boards with relatives; free to relocate.
Hobbies: Golf; tennis; music appreciation.

(FOR AMPLIFICATION PLEASE SEE FOLLOWING)

Uncluttered record demonstrating capabilities through satisfactory discharge of variety of duties assigned in variety of employments. Second amplified employment enters risky area of personal reason for leaving as later developments appear to justify action.

Amplified Resume   Roberta J. Read

EMPLOYMENT HIGHLIGHTS

1978–Present
KAUFMAN DISTRIBUTING CO.

Employed to handle single-girl office. Does bookkeeping, prepares monthly statements, handles correspondence (some by dictation, balance on own initiative), checks invoices, watches overdue accounts, takes phone calls.

Reason for desiring change: Greater income.

1975–1978
ALDERSON & WERDER

Employed as one of five personnel in her type work; moved rapidly to top. Duties consisted of taking rough drafts of audits, putting them in final report form, typing and lithographing them when required. Was called on to proofread work of others in the group. Had so excellent a grasp of office detail, when supervisor left unexpectedly, was asked to instruct the replacement supervisor in office procedures.

Resentment of new supervisor to conscientious attempts to familiarize her with office operations made for a difficult situation and resulted in Miss Read's resignation. Shortly thereafter aforementioned supervisor was asked to resign.

1971–1975
MURRAY PERSONNEL SERVICE

Employed as Personnel Clerk and Typist-Secretary with responsibility for the following:

1) Interviewing applicants; arranging for aptitude tests, advising on results.
2) Maintaining files of results and eligibilities.
3) Correspondence (notification of applicants, etc.).
4) Setting up interview appointments.

In addition to standard office duties and specific duties outlined above, was charged with function of requisitioning necessary forms and supplies necessary for general office operation.

Reason for leaving: To accept better paying position in area which would permit her to board with relatives.

GENERAL
Has left each position voluntarily to improve status; excellent letters of reference from former employers. Please no contact with present employers until after interview.

Synopsis of Resume of: 17 Orchard Place
IRWIN E. DAILEY   Houston, TX 77006
                                                Phone: (713) 514−7443

JOB OBJECTIVE

Position as Production Control Manager

EMPLOYMENT

1975–Present   **PRODUCTION CONTROL SUPERINTENDENT**
                Ames Lumber Products Corporation
                Houston, TX

1971–1975   **SENIOR STAFF CONSULTANT**
                Swenson Mgmt. Advisory Consultants, Inc.
                98 East 14th St., Chicago Heights, IL

1956–1971   **HEAD OF PLANNING** (moved up through stages from machinist)
                Clinton Machine Co., Columbus, OH

EDUCATION

1952–1956   Tiffin University, Tiffin, OH
                    Degree: B.S. in Commerce
                    Expenses: Earned approximately 50%.
                    Honors: Dean's List last 2 semesters.
                    Note: Employment during college precluded extracurricular
                               activities.

Other: Clinton Machine Company: Mgmt. courses; IBM courses. Yearly
                seminars in San Francisco, CA, sponsored by present company.

PERSONAL

Born: 8/10/34 in Chicago, IL. Height 5'11"; wt. 180 lbs.
Married: 2 children in college.
Health: Good; no physical limitations.
Hobbies: Hunting; Swimming; Golf.
Affiliations: American Production & Control Society;
                Chamber of Commerce.

(FOR AMPLIFICATION PLEASE SEE FOLLOWING)
*Solid background picture achieved through specifics of present position, as well as through general detail
of former ones. Reasons for desiring to leave excellent position were of personal nature, better explained at
interview.*

Amplified Resume   Irwin E. Dailey

EMPLOYMENT

1975–Present
AMES LUMBER PRODUCTS CORP.

Employed as Production Control Manager with the specific assignment of establishing a 3 plant unified corporate production control organization.

Organization was completed, tying in sales forecasts on stock and special orders, outside warehousing on nationwide basis, with proper stocks for prompt customer service, scheduling of production and shipments, and appropriate raw material purchasing. Task complicated by rapid company growth (from 3 to 6 plants and individual plant company growth).

In 1977 a crash decentralization was begun, with an independent department in each of 6 plants. Was made Production Control Superintendent of headquarters plant in Houston, Texas. Established model department to be followed by other plants. Departments were separate except for stock warehouse inventory tie in.

Now directs a 110 man department controlling the following: scheduling, order processing, shipping, traffic, receiving, warehousing, inventory control and purchasing, for a 900 man plant with productive volume in substantial 7 figures.

Results: 1. Men trained in corporate setup have taken over other plants; men presently in training at Houston slated for department head positions.

2. All standards set by management have been met or exceeded; low turnover of dept. personnel.

3. Rewarded for efforts by 12% salary increase.

Reason for desiring change: To be discussed at interview.

1971–1975
SWENSON MGMT. ADVISORY CONSULTANTS INC.

Originally employed as Staff Consultant; in 6 months promoted to Senior Staff Consultant.

Analyzed and evaluated client problems and capabilities; recommended corrective measures; took proper action where recommendations were accepted. Assignments were in all sections of the United States as well as Mexico. Clients were primarily major companies in a variety of fields: insurance, ship building, manufacturing, etc.

(continued)

Amplified Resume   Irwin E. Dailey

1971–1975 employment continued

Varied problems encompassed the following:

1. Industrial Engineering.
2. Inventory and Production Control.
3. Spot Trouble Shooting.
4. Mgmt., personnel and organization appraisal.
5. Plant layout with materials handling and warehousing.
6. Layout and planning of facilities for new home office bldg.
7. Complete plant analysis.

Reason for change:
Although efforts rewarded by slightly less than 50% salary increase, felt excessive long distance travel precluded normal family life; resigned.

1956–1971
CLINTON MACHINE COMPANY

Employed as machinist; promoted through machine inspection, assembly, shop scheduling to Head of Planning.

During illness or vacation absences of superiors, acted as Chief Industrial Engineer and Plant Manager.

Reason for change:

To increase income and broaden experience.

REFERENCES

Available

Synopsis of:
MICHAEL SIMMONS

6440 Oregon St.
Ft. Myers, FL 33901
Phone: (813) 297–5590

JOB OBJECTIVE

PRODUCTION MANAGER

1978–Present	Production Manager WXLF-TV, Ft. Myers, FL
1977–1978	Production Manager WAEO, Rhinelander, WI
1973–1977	Chief, Information Division. United States Army
Part-time	Summer jobs: Radiographer, Pipeweld X-ray Corp. Free-lance copywriting, sundry advertising firms.

EDUCATION

1968–1973	Syracuse University, Syracuse, NY Degree: B.S. in Broadcasting
Other:	Northeast Broadcasting School, Boston, MA

PERSONAL

Born:	1948 in Lansing, MI. Height 6'2"; weight 197.
Married:	2 children (pre-school age).
Health:	Excellent; no physical limitations.
Hobbies:	Writing; woodworking; hi-fi; swimming; golf.
Affiliations:	Writers Club; Palmaire Golf Club.

(FOR AMPLIFICATION PLEASE SEE FOLLOWING)

Amplified Resume   Michael Simmons

June 1978 –Present
WXLF-TV, Ft. Myers, FL

Employed as Production Manager of new television station not yet on the air. Had full responsibility for initial airdate preparation; in full charge of all production following airdate. Included: newscasts, commercial announcement, programs and administrative details.

Due to small staff, assumed additional duties of program director, continuity writer, staff announcer, as well as assisting photographer. Despite understaffing and limited technical equipment, organized an efficient, smooth running unit resulting in the new station moving up in national network ratings well beyond the expectations for a new station in a comparable time period.

Reason for desiring change:

Prefer larger, established station, where efforts may be concentrated in production area.

January 1977–June 1978
WAEO, Rhinelander, WI

Hired as continuity writer; promoted in two months to Production Director. Had full responsibility for all commercial production and attendant details.

Reason for leaving:

Amicable separation to accept present position.

1973–1977
United States Army

Chief, Information Division; qualified in one-third normal time due to self-training on own time and initiative. Special accomplishments included:
(1) Wrote, narrated, filmed and directed half-hour color documentary.
(2) Provided news releases; filmed and supplied news film to national news services.
(3) Had sole responsibility for any news released from base.

REFERENCES

On Request

Synopsis of Resume of:
MELVIN J. HAMILTON

879 Wiltshire Rd.
Lowell, MA 01835
Phone: (617) 986—4966

JOB OBJECTIVE

Programming or supervisory position.

EMPLOYMENT RECORD

10/78—2/80	Coordinating & Scheduling Analyst Martin Co., Lowell, MA. Mfr. of helicopters.
7/75—9/78	Systems Analyst Curtiss Electronics Corp. Mfr. electronic equipment. Boston, MA
6/73—6/75	Group Leader (Computer Operations) General Copy Corp., Boston, MA
1971—1973	Senior Computer Operator Newark Power Co., Newark, NJ.

EDUCATION

1967—1970	University of Rochester, Rochester, NY B.S. Degree.
Other:	Knowledge of COBOL and FORTRAN.

PERSONAL

Born:	1949 in Burlington, VT. Height 5'11"; wt. 175 lbs.
Married:	Wife a college graduate; 4 children, age range: 5 - preschool.
Health:	Excellent; no physical limitations; last physical 12/79.
Finances:	Good order; owns home; will relocate for exceptional opportunity.
Hobbies:	Sailing; bridge; boat building.
Affiliations:	Lowell Yacht Club; Chamber of Commerce; U of R. Alumni Ass'n.
Service:	Member National Guard.

(FOR AMPLIFICATION PLEASE SEE FOLLOWING)
Specialized field where specifics are essential as to training and equipment familiarization.

Amplified Resume   Page 2

EMPLOYMENT RECORD

10/78–2/80
MARTIN CO.

Employed as Coordinating and Scheduling Analyst with following responsibilities: projecting future machine schedules, coordinating new systems in operations sections, explaining new procedures to operating sections.

Helped install a new numbering system for reports and machine runs; assigned reports and run number to new, recurring, or one-time job. Required to have full knowledge of each system as to operation and purpose.

Duties included statistical work for operations supervisor. Developed figures for management (budget, rental, machine usage, etc).

Indication of company evaluation: $700 per year increase in starting salary.

Reason for leaving: Voluntary resignation to seek position in systems work and gain experience in programming.

7/75–9/78
CURTISS ELECTRONICS CORP.

Employed as Systems Analyst. Developed system for customer requirements; priced system for profitable, successful bid. Wrote customer contracts; attended bidders conferences.

Followed operations closely to insure fulfillment of contractual requirements. Made monthly financial evaluations of each contract; evaluated existing systems.

Reason for leaving: Offer from Martin Co. which appeared to have greater potential.

6/73–6/75
GENERAL COPY CORP.

Employed as Group Leader. Supervised 6 personnel in the operation and continuous flow of work through computers for daily periods from 3:00 p.m. to 12:00 p.m.

Continuation of work flow from day shift was maintained. Included such standard items as accounts payable and receivable, payroll, billing, etc.

(continued)

Amplified Resume   Page 3

GENERAL COPY CORP. employment cont'd.

If trouble developed was entirely on own responsibility to determine cause and implement solution.

Company indicated appreciation of efforts by substantial salary increase.

Reason for leaving: Amicable separation to accept position next above which did not require night work.

1971–1973
NEWARK POWER CO. (Utility)

Employed as trainee on data processing equipment.
Promoted steadily to final post of Senior Computer Operator.

Operated and wired machines listed; completed work for financial statements on wide variety of subjects (labor, materials, transportation, etc.). In final year gained experience as operator and programmer for the new card system computer.

Indication of company evaluation of services: $3,000 increase in yearly salary.

Reason for leaving: To accept better paying position next above.

REFERENCES

Available on request at interview.

Synopsis of Resume of:
PATRICIA KENT

9972 Lone Tree
Dallas, TX 75218
Phone: (214) 382–4391

JOB OBJECTIVE

Public Affairs Director

EMPLOYMENT

1977–Present   Public Affairs Director; talk show hostess; reporter
WXTN-TV, Dallas, TX

1973–1977   WYND, Slidell, LA
Traffic and continuity director.

1972–1973   WQED-TV, Houston, TX
Production Assistant.

1969–1972   WVIZ, Cleveland, OH
Continuity and production

EDUCATION

1965–1969   Ohio State University
Major: Journalism
Minor: Communications media

Other: New York University
Summer workshop in radio and television
Dallas Advertising Club
Public Relations Seminar

Languages: Spanish (fluent), French (working knowledge).

PERSONAL

Born: 1947 in Cleveland, OH. Marital status: single.
Appearance: Height 5'8"; weight 115. Health: excellent.
Hobbies: Swimming; scuba; sewing; puppetry; art; painting.
Affiliations: Dallas Press Club; Museum Director; Ecology Committee;
(present)   Professional Women's Club.
(Past)   Chairperson for Dallas Symphony Charity Ball, local telethon, March
of Dimes, Slidell Civic Association.

(FOR AMPLIFICATION PLEASE SEE FOLLOWING)
Although jobs frequently changed, progression in salary and responsibilities make logical sequence.
Emphasis on affiliations to strengthen qualifications for objective.

Amplified Resume   Patricia Kent

EMPLOYMENT

1977–Present
WXNT-TV, Dallas TX

Employed as member of News Department assigned to special features. Included civic and cultural events, politics, and soft news items. Required to shoot, process and edit film, write and produce audio commentary.

Upon resignation of talk show host, was given opportunity to be hostess of the live show station presented daily as a public relations and community project. Given full responsibility for the hour show. Designed set, created opening and close, procured clothing sponsor to furnish daily wardrobe, lined up and scheduled all guests. Guests are briefed slightly, but prefers spontaneity of the largely unrehearsed interview. Guests have included: U.S. senators, visiting actors and celebrities, as well as concerned citizens within the station's viewing area.

Recently given title of "Public Affairs Director;" responsibilities in addition to those above include moderating panel discussions and special programs on various issues.

Reason for desiring change: Salary not in line with increased responsibilities.

1973–1977
WYND, Slidell, LA

Employed as receptionist with agreement for transfer to production department when vacancy occurred. An earlier opening in traffic department offered and accepted. Responsible for daily log as well as continuity; wrote commercial copy and station promotional material. In addition, did occasional on-air psots and voice-overs; filled in for "Romper Room" hostess when needed.

Reason for leaving: Offer of more interesting position.

1972–1973
WQED-TV (Educational)

Employed as production assistant, designed sets and graphics; served as liaison between the technical and instructional personnel. Left for better paying job above.

1969–1972

Employed as production assistant for the city's then new educational television station. Duties proved to be primarily in the traffic area (daily logs and program guides). Amicable separation to seek position with more production emphasis.

REFERENCES ON REQUEST

Synopsis of Resume of:
NANCY W. MITCHELL

33 Rand Place
Atlanta, GA 30315
Phone: (404) 897–9641

JOB OBJECTIVE

Field of Public Relations - Promotion - Advertising.

EDUCATION

High School: Westover School, Middlebury, CT
                Graduated 1970.
                President French Club; Captain Sr. Tennis Team.

College: Mt. Holyoke College, South Hadley, MA
                Graduated 1974. Degree: A.B. Major: English.
                Assistant Editor college publication.

Other: "Experiment in International Living" - 6 wks. 1970.
                Competitive program. Selection of young Americans
                to represent U.S. in foreign countries. Selection on
                basis of: scholastic achievement, mental alertness,
                physical fitness, personality and character. Assigned
                to group going to France; spent 6 weeks with French family.

                Has traveled extensively; speaks French fluently.

EMPLOYMENT

11/76–Present   KYKA-TV, 890 So. Main St., Atlanta, GA
                Promotion Writer with multiple additional responsibilities.

10/75–11/76   MATHER ADVERTISING INC. Radio & TV Advertising.
                70 Stone St., Boston, MA
                Secretarial and general office work.

8/74–10/75   WYKB, 905 Commercial St., Boston, MA
                Secretary to Program Director

PERSONAL

Born: 1/20/52 in Charleston, SC. Height 5′9″; wt. 126 lbs.
Health: Excellent. Marital status: widow. No children.
Hobbies: Tennis; golf; music (accomplished pianist).
Residence: Apartment; willing to relocate anywhere in U.S.

(FOR AMPLIFICATION PLEASE SEE FOLLOWING)
Field in which superior education is likely to carry more weight than average experience would; therefore, former is given synopsis page preference.

Amplified Resume

EMPLOYMENT

11/76–Present
KYKA-TV, Atlanta, GA

As promotion writer is responsible for all on-the-air promotion (30 sec., 60 sec., etc.) for each day's log. A major TV station, spots and promotions are extensive, requiring speed and good organization in meeting deadlines, in addition to creative writing ability. Is also responsible for all trailers, tapes, slides and videotape. Checks and processes them on arrival; screens them for use. Entails determination of what will be used, discarded, or cut, as well as instructing film department on proper cutting procedure to attain desired length and content.

In clerical area, is required to log all promotional announcements, check traffic boards and maintain Kardex file. Makes out promotion orders, promotion reports, program schedules, and distributes to proper departments. Makes periodic program checks to insure information is correct and current.

Reason for desiring change: Feels duties too general; would like position with more clearly defined responsibilities.

10/75–11/76
MATHER ADVERTISING INC., Boston, MA

Employed for secretarial and office work. In short period responsibilities broadened to include radio and television copy and limited account servicing. Office packaged several shows affording opportunity to gain valuable experience in this area, in addition to public relations and agency media work.

Reason for leaving: To return south to be nearer immediate family on death of husband.

8/74–10/75
WYKB, Boston, MA

Employed as Secretary to Program Director. Standard secretarial responsibilities encompassed typing, correspondence, and operation of the following machines: verifax, mimeograph, TWX, switchboard.

Specific duties included the following:
1. Maintenance program schedules.
2. Coordinating public service & program promotion announcements.
3. Operations detail for all commercial shows and spots - schedules, production materials and copy.

Reason for leaving: To gain experience in advertising field.

REFERENCES AVAILABLE

Synopsis of Resume of:
PETER DIXON

45 Barnes Ave.
Memphis, TN 38118
Phone: (901) 863−2819

JOB OBJECTIVE

Purchasing Agent or position leading to it in near future.

EMPLOYMENT

2/77−Present	**NATIONAL DYNAMICS CORPORATION** 1800 Cruger Ave., Memphis, TN Buyer - Mechanical Components
9/72−2/77	**LEWIN MFG. CO.** (Office furniture & supplies) 1328 Taft Ave., Atlanta, GA General Purchasing Agent.
11/71−9/72	**SCHULTZ FABRICATORS** (Plastic fabricators) East Atlanta, GA Purchasing Agent.
11/63−11/71	**WHITE CO. INC.** (Hospital equip. mfr's.) Nashville, TN Metals Buyer.
8/47−11/63	**NEWTON LAUNDRY MACHINERY CO.** Union St., Indianapolis, IN Assistant Traffic Manager.

EDUCATION

1943−1947 Evening School:	Brothers Institute, Indianapolis, IN. Graduated.
1951−53	Jefferson Institute, Indianapolis, IN. Machine Shop course.
1966	Alva Technical School, Nashville, TN. Chemistry (1 yr. course).
1971−72	Atlanta Institute of Technology. Industrial Mgmt. course
1976	Memphis Tech. Metallurgy (1 yr. course).

PERSONAL

Born:	5/30/25 in Indianapolis, IN. Single.
Health:	Good; no physical limitations; last physical - 1979.
Appearance:	Height 6'; weight 195 lbs.
Hobbies:	Sports (spectator and participation); duplicate bridge.
Affiliations:	American Society for Metals.

(FOR AMPLIFICATION PLEASE SEE FOLLOWING)
Type of material purchased is mentioned, as well as approximate size of company, to show applicant's level of purchase responsibility. Yearly income (despite increases) in low bracket, therefore mention of it is avoided.

Amplified Resume

Peter Dixon

EMPLOYMENT

2/79–Present
NATIONAL DYNAMICS CORPORATION (approx. 2,000 employees)

Employed as Buyer of Mechanical Components in the Electronics Division, with an expediter and stenographer under his direction. Operates on own responsibility, locates suppliers, issues orders without supervision. Nearly all work in the division is on government contract with time and quality paramount; consequently, his object is to obtain materials consistently up to specifications from firms who can be depended upon for delivery.

Travels to vendors' plants throughout the United States to check facilities; keeps records which are referred to when placing orders. Reads blueprints; interprets production orders to insure delivery of materials in proper sequence, avoiding holdups in production.

Purchases such materials as: panels, springs, hinges, chassis, metal cabinets. Familiar with metals and plastics, and accustomed to ordering to extremely close tolerances. Replaced two buyers (metal components and hardware) and has done the work of both.

Results:
Consistently received proper material with very low percentage of rejects. Ten buyers were recommended for salary increases at last evaluation period; was one of two selected for the increase. Yearly income has risen by $4,850 since start.

Reason for change: To accept better position.

9/72–2/77
LEWIN MFG. COMPANY (approx. 700 employees)

As General Purchasing Agent was responsible for the entire purchase activity. Four buyers, 3 stenographers and a clerk under his direction. Purchases were in substantial 7 figures, from vendors in southern and mid western U.S.

Reason for leaving: Was given no authority to run his department. Held responsible for acts of subordinates, but could not enforce his orders to them. Resigned when situation became intolerable.

11/71–9/72
SCHULTZ FABRICATORS (approx. 300 employees)

General Purchasing Agent, also in charge of inventory control. Record was such was approached by above firm and offered better paying, more responsible position. Resigned to accept.

(continued)

Amplified Resume

Peter Dixon

**11/63–11/71
WHITE CO. INC. (approx. 800 employees)**

Employed as metals buyer with the added responsibility for return and replacement of all defective materials of all types. Because of type of equipment produced, metals were highly specialized and required to meet variety of unusual conditions. Mr. Dixon maintained noteworthy record of never having a machine down for lack of materials.

Reason for change: Merger of company eliminated position.

**8/47–11/63
NEWTON LAUNDRY MACHINERY CO. (approx 500 employees)**

Employed as errand boy; worked into stock clerk, then into an assisting position in: Stores, Purchasing and Receiving. Substituted for absentees, and filled in when work load was heavy in any section.

In 1957 promoted to Assistant Traffic Manager, responsible for shipment of all materials by every transportation means (rail, truck, express and air).

Reason for change: Resigned to accept position with substantially greater financial return.

GENERAL

Has a knowledge of factory operation gained from inside. Is an able workman (built home from ground up - wired it, and had it accepted by Underwriters). Can grasp and solve problems, matching procurement to production.

REFERENCES

Available on request

Synopsis of Resume of:
VALERIE CORNWALL

46 Charles St.
New York City, NY 10014
Phone: (212) 214–7596

OBJECTIVE

Receptionist and Model (Size 10)

EXPERIENCE

1978–Present   **RECEPTIONIST AND MODEL**
Fashion Frolics, Inc. (Mfr's. ladies' dresses)
770 Seventh Ave., New York, NY

1975–1978   Receptionist and Switchboard Operator
Williams Printing Co.
311 South St., Memphis, TN

1973–1975   Sales Clerk
Diamond Dept. Store
10 Fifth Ave., Memphis, TN

EDUCATION

High School: South Morgan High School, Nashville, TN
Graduated 1973.

Modeling School: Royal Modeling School, 500 Fifth Ave., New York, NY
One year course (completed).

PERSONAL

Born: 8/6/55 in Nashville, TN. Marital status: single.
Appearance: 5'7"; wt. 115.
Health: Excellent, no physical limitations.
Residence: Rent apartment; own car.
Hobbies: Ballet dancing; dramatics; music.

(FOR AMPLIFICATION PLEASE SEE FOLLOWING)
Shows steady progression and experience in field of job objective, plus strong desire and reason for wishing to remain in present locality.

Amplified Resume   Valerie Cornwall

EMPLOYMENT HIGHLIGHTS

1978–Present
FASHION FROLICS, INC.

Acted as receptionist for firm, screening all callers; made appointments; acted as liaison between representatives from buying offices and salesmen. Modeled dresses. Although this was to have been a minor function, it is now a major one, with corresponding pay increase.

Reason for desiring change: Thoroughly enjoys work; however, company will relocate in Hollywood, California in near future. Offered position in new location. Declined, wishes to remain in New York City.

1975–1978
WILLIAMS PRINTING CO.

Doubled as switchboard operator and receptionist for company specializing in printing of fine letterheads, statements, etc. Familiarized self with company operation to intelligently answer customer and potential customer inquiries.

Reason for leaving: Offered raise to remain; wished to relocate in New York City.

1973–1975
DIAMOND DEPT. STORE

Employed as sales clerk in ladies' ready-to-wear. On several occasions was selected to model coats and sweaters throughout the store, and to participate in store fashion shows.

Reason for leaving: Increase in salary.

GENERAL

Able to procure excellent letters of reference from present and previous employers if required, or they may be contacted by any prospective employer.

Resume of:
CHERYL LARSON

9009 Fox St.
Denver, CO 80204
Phone: (303) 874–7588

JOB OBJECTIVE

Position in Cardio-Pulmonary Department. Flexible, willing to learn through new experiences and advanced studies in present or related fields.

EDUCATION

1979–1980   Hillsview Junior College, Colorado Springs, CO.
Assoc. degree in Respiratory Therapy.
Courses included:
Airway Management, Artificial Ventilation Therapy, Cardiopulmonary Resuscitation, Chest Physiotherapy, General Patient Care.

1978–Present   St. Joseph Hospital, Denver, CO.
Classroom and laboratory training augmented with hospital orientation. Started as Respiratory Therapy Technician Trainee, in work-job program.

EMPLOYMENT

1978–Present   St. Joseph Hospital (same as above)
Employed part-time as Respiratory Therapy Tech. III.

Performs respiratory therapy and EKG duties: ventilator installation, blood tests, pulmonary function studies, breathing treatments.

Active on "Code Blue" team. Gives outpatient instruction on proper breathing techniques; attends emergency pacemaker placement; assists in stress testing and holter-monitor fitting.

PERSONAL

Age: 23   Born 3/10/58 in Aspen, Colorado. Height 5′4″; wt. 110 lbs.
Health: Excellent. Marital status: single. Free for flexible hours.
Hobbies: Skiing; biking; hiking; camping; reading.
Affiliations: Denver Ski Club; Young Republicans.

REFERENCES

On Request

(Student record with limited employment and good training, has more punch by deleting synopsis. Note her good physical dimensions, which are used to bring "word snapshot" into keener focus.)

Synopsis of Resume of:
HARRY KRAMER

12 Shoreham Park
Denver, CO 80290
Phone: (303) 297-4292

JOB OBJECTIVE

Overall Restaurant Management (Food & Beverage).

EMPLOYMENT

(Note: dated employments shown below were selected to show experience in many areas of restaurant and bar operation, following 3 years of apprenticeship in Hofbrau House (Hotel) in Stuttgart, Germany, where he received thorough and complete European training.)

8/27/76–Present   ASSISTANT CHEF (20 kitchen personnel)
White Horse Motor Inn & Restaurant
Mountain View Rd., Denver, CO

1972–1974   MGR. FOOD PREPARATION FOR COLLEGE STUDENTS
Westover College, Sundale, MI
(Employed by Corbett Co., 60 Fisher Bldg. Detroit, MI)

9/69–11/71   CHIEF STEWARD
Detroit German Club, Stillson St., Detroit, MI

1965–1969   CHEF (Heavy food preparation - no short orders)
Golden Diner, 1700 Main St., Detroit, MI

1964–1965   SUPERVISING CHEF (party and volume luncheon business)
Hilltop Restaurant, Broad St., Detroit, MI

1958–1964   CHEF STEWARD (purchased for bar and restaurant)
Duane Co., Baytown Hotel, Baytown, L.I., NY

1954–1958   SELF EMPLOYED (purchased, remodeled, operated)
Longport Hotel, Old Forge, NY

PERSONAL

Age: Born 2/27/27 in Raleigh, NC. Widower.
Appearance: Height 5'11"; weight 184 lbs.
Health: Good; no physical limitations; last physical - 1979.
Residence: Rents apartment; free to relocate.
Hobbies: Music; Travel; Painting.

(FOR EMPLOYMENT DETAIL & EDUCATION PLEASE SEE FOLLOWING)
Only principal jobs are listed to spotlight skills and wide range of experience. Interim jobs were of lesser importance and to list them would serve no real purpose. "General" sums up overall record, which can (and probably will) be discussed in full at interview.

Amplified Resume   Harry Kramer

EMPLOYMENT HIGHLIGHTS

8/76–Present
WHITE HORSE MOTOR INN & RESTAURANT
(Serves 1,500 meals per day with varied menus;
single breakfasts to large banquets)

Employed as Assistant Chef. Supervises overall operation of the kitchen in normal operation. Lays out daily work schedules for 20 personnel; personally prepares all sauces and specialized European dishes for this quality restaurant (considered to be one of the top restaurants in Denver and surrounding area).

In spite of insistance on discipline and refusal to settle for less than best efforts, personnel turnover has been lower than average for restaurants of similar class. Personal record is such, present employer may be contacted for reference.

Reason for change: Desires to move up to top position.

1972–1974
CORBETT COMPANY

Employed by Corbett Co. (contractors for cafeteria and restaurant operation) to manage the student feeding operation at the Westover College, located in the suburbs of Lansing, Michigan. Planned and scheduled menus; purchased all supplies; hired and trained necessary personnel (usually students - consequently required manipulation of manpower schedules to fit class schedules). In addition, kept all records and did own bookkeeping.

Paid per student rate by college, but operated on a cost plus basis rebating difference (if any) to the school. Under his management, restaurant so well operated alumni dinners were held there for the first time. This allowed extra profit, with the end result that refunds were made to the college every month of operation; reached maximum of $4,000 for a single month.

Record resulted in transfer to Detroit into the Auto Dealers Institute. Proved to be industrial type cafeteria operation, utilizing but small portion of his extensive training and skill.

Reason for change: Resigned to seek more suitable post.

9/69–11/71
DETROIT GERMAN CLUB

Employed as Chief Steward in charge of all restaurant activity including purchasing. Developed steady banquet and special dinner business which returned substantial profit to club and paid for extensive club improvements.

Reason for change: Resigned to seek position with more potential.

Amplified Resume

Harry Kramer

EMPLOYMENT HIGHLIGHTS continued

PRIOR

Posts included:

(1) Baytown Hotel, Baytown, L.I., NY. Complete charge of purchasing and operation for bar and restaurant doing monthly dollar volume of $60,000. Returned solid profit to owners. Letters of Recommendation.

(2) Self employed in build up, repair and operation of Longport Hotel, which is still in operation at Old Forge, NY. Sold at good profit.

EDUCATION

1945–48   Presbyterian College of North Carolina
Courses leading to Business Administration degree.
(Left voluntarily to enter food field).

1948–51   Hofbrau Hotel, Stuttgart, Germany
3 year apprenticeship.

1951–54   Five country experience as Journeyman to qualify for official designation, "Qualified Cook".

GENERAL

Has consistently made money for owners in each employment. Offers wide range of experience in large and small operations, in bar, restaurant, cafeteria and commissary direction. Has letters attesting to complete satisfaction given in various positions; left each position voluntarily.

Poised, competent manner, a direct approach and pleasing personality. Desires permanent position fully utilizing his experience, capabilities, and specialized training, with growth potential.

REFERENCES

Available on Request. Letters referred to
above available for review at interview.

Synopsis of Resume of:
FRED G. SNOW

418 West St.
Pittsburgh, PA 15235
Phone: (412) 303–6224

JOB OBJECTIVE

Position in retail management field. Department store or comparable operation.

EMPLOYMENT

12/79–Present   MERCHANDISING MANAGER
R. S. Wilson Department Store
West Broadway, Pittsburgh, PA

2/67–12/79   STORE MANAGER (final position)
Ward Roebuck & Co., NY
Yearly income increased to $20,000 during employment.

1965–1967   Station attendant - Oklahoma Oil Company
Allentown, PA

1963–1965   Part time during school years:
drug store clerk, grocery delivery, etc.

EDUCATION

High School: Lincoln High School, Providence, RI

College: Carnegie Business College, Pittsburgh, PA
2 year course in Business Management included:
Accounting, Auditing, Finance.

PERSONAL

Age: Born 12/6/45. Married, no children.
Appearance: Height 6'; weight 190 lbs.
Health: Good; last physical 1980.
Residence: Rents; free to relocate.
Affiliations: American Legion; YMCA.
Hobbies: Badminton; golf; swimming.

(FOR AMPLIFICATION SEE FOLLOWING)

School dates not mentioned as they were broken up and would serve only to confuse the issue. Salary mentioned in previous rather than present employment to alert prospective employer to earning bracket without pinpointing amount. Strongly stated reason for leaving present employment (which had been of about 5 mos. duration) could be risky if previous employment record did not indicate applicant's reliability.

Amplified Resume   Fred G. Snow

EMPLOYMENT DETAILS

12/79–Present
R. S. WILSON DEPARTMENT STORE

Employed as Merchandise Manager with complete responsibility for all merchandising for entire store (composed of approximately 50 depts.).

Has situation well in hand and functioning smoothly; however, disagrees with company policies which he considers antiquated. Would make a change to a more aggressive company.

2/67–12/79
WARD ROEBUCK & COMPANY

Originally employed as sales clerk in the Housewares Dept. of the company store in Providence, RI.

Promoted after 2 weeks to Manager of the Mens' and Boys' Clothing Department.

Promoted after one and one half years to Assistant Manager of a store with an operating personnel of 50.

Promoted after one year to Assistant Manager in Charge of Operations at the company's larger store in Boston, MA. Had charge of all operational functions.

Promoted after 2 years to Store Manager at Allentown, PA, a store with personnel of 35. After 18 months moved as Manager to a larger store (double the volume), at Scranton, PA. In 10 months increased volume by 35% and was rated "Potential District Manager" material. As part of a planned program leading to such a position was:

Promoted to Regional Merchandiser for 115 stores, with supervision of: (1) Women's Ready-to-Wear, (2) Domestic and Yard Goods, (3) Mens' and Boys' Hosiery, (4) Curtains and Drapes.

As a second step in the sequence, after a year was moved to the large store in Baltimore, MD, as Manager. Store employed from 100 to 125 persons at various seasons. Managed store from June 1974 to April 1977. Despite national downward trend during that period, increased store's volume on a yearly basis over $350,000. Built an excellent record on turnover of personnel as well as housekeeping.

Reason for change: Received what appeared to be an excellent offer from R.S. Wilson Dept. Store and, with the idea of broadening his experience, accepted.

REFERENCES AVAILABLE

Synopsis of Resume of:
HUGH MC SWEENEY

20 Aspin Place
Colorado Springs, CO 80906
Phone: (303) 644–7660

JOB OBJECTIVE

Position in field of sales.

EMPLOYMENT

12/76–Present	SALES REPRESENTATIVE (Eastern Colorado) Universal Metals Inc., 490 E. 37th St., Denver, CO
2/72–12/76	FIELD MANAGER (promoted from salesman) Lifetime Cookware Inc. Oklahoma City, OK
1970–1/72	DRIVER-SALESMAN (stores, hotels, restaurants) Kelsey Bakery Inc., Yukon, OK
Prior	Part time and summer employment during school period: (1) paper route from age 10 to 16; (2) vendor at athletic events.

EDUCATION

	McQuid High School, Lawton, OK Graduated. Advertising Mgr. for yearbook.

1966–1970	University of Maryland (branch)
	    Courses given by professor on military
	    base included: American History, English
	    Literature, English.

Misc:	Passed 2 year college level test while in service.

PERSONAL

Born:	8/10/48 in Lawton, OK. Height 6′; wt. 190 lbs.
Married:	Wife R.N.; 3 children, ages: 6 and preschool.
Health:	Good; no physical limitations; last physical - 1979.
Hobbies:	Golf; skiing; family activities.
Affiliations:	Toastmasters Club; Rotary.
Civic:	Chairman of Civil Defense Committee; with others, currently forming Air, Sea, Rescue Group.
'66–'70 Service:	USA. Served in Germany. Hon. Discharge; not in Reserve.

(FOR AMPLIFICATION PLEASE SEE FOLLOWING)
Showing sales resume essentials; what sold, where, to whom, how long, how much.

Amplified Resume   Hugh Mc Sweeney

EMPLOYMENT HIGHLIGHTS

12/76–Present
UNIVERSAL METALS INC.
(Distributors: metal moldings, floor covering and allied products.
Nationally advertised brands.)

Employed as sales representative in 10 counties, including Colorado Springs. Calls on retailers, department stores, lumber companies, fabricators of practically all description, in addition to floor covering specialty stores. Operates almost entirely on his own with minimum assistance from home office.

Assists retail accounts by setting up displays, working out cooperative advertising programs, or incentive rebates based on volume. Organizes promotions such as VINYLCO street stripping. Women employed in these promotions demonstrate easy clean-up quality of the stripping, in addition to passing out literature and small give-away items.

Collection (to a limited degree) comes within the framework of his responsibilities. Has demonstrated tact in this difficult area, effecting collections from delinquent customers in manner allowing retention of account.

In common with all other company men, faced problem of 35% total volume company loss when VINYLCO slipped badly nationally.

Results

1. Although last man hired, was retained with enlarged territory when sales force cut.

2. Increased sales volume on ceramic tile by over 40% (major item).

3. Increased sales of vinyl floor covering by over 20%.

4. Added over 50 new accounts in highly competitive market.

5. Company evaluation of services indicated by $8,500 increase in yearly income since start of employment.

Reason for desiring change:

Although offered substantial increase to remain, feels further company growth improbable. Separation amicable; has given month's notice; company may be contacted for reference and substantiation of above record.

Amplified Resume   Hugh Mc Sweeney

2/72–12/76
LIFETIME COOKWARE INC.

Employed as door-to-door salesman in Oklahoma City, OK, office. 1973 became top producing salesman of the 53 in the Oklahoma City branch, 8th of the entire 1200 route district.

Promoted to Field Manager, 1974. Completed special training and given area consisting of El Paso, Lincoln, Elbert counties, and surrounding counties.

Hired, trained and supervised 20 salesmen. Approximately one-quarter of men he developed have entered, or are currently being trained for, management positions.

Results: Increased sales volume for entire area by 32% in 1976 (last full year as manager).

Reason for leaving:
To accept better position above.

1970–1/72
KELSEY BAKERY INC.

As driver-salesman, called on stores, hotels and restaurants in Yukon, Oklahoma and surrounding area. Assumed established but non-productive route. Through courteous, efficient, reliable service, built customer volume and confidence to point he was permitted to telephone key accounts for their requirements in advance of his personal call. This enabled proper products to be carried on a given day in proper amounts, resulting in full customer satisfaction.

Results: During period of employment, commission (based on sales volume) showed just short of 65% increase.

Awarded "Top Cookie" trophy, given in recognition of outstanding sales volume increase.

Reason for leaving:
To accept better paying position above.

REFERENCES

Available

Synopsis of Resume of: 987 Culver Ave.
DUDLEY M. HOWARD   Burlington, VT 05401
                                                           Phone: (802) 749-9817

JOB OBJECTIVE

Position in Sales Mgmt. on District or Regional level.

EMPLOYMENT

8/79–Present	Haley Chevrolet Company, Burlington, VT Appraiser and salesman (interim work while seeking suitable position)
1976–8/79	Mansfield Motors (Ford Agency), Rutland, VT Sales Manager
1972–1976	Rutland Motor Sales (Oldsmobile Agency), Rutland, VT Salesman
1968–1972	Valley Ford, Inc. (Ford sales and service) Shrewsburg, VT Service Mgr.
1959–1968	Lakeport Marine Company, Lakeport, NH Salesman

EDUCATION

Formal:	Rockland High School, Rockland, ME. State University of Maine, Orono, ME. Business Administration. Left voluntarily for financial reasons. Activities: advertising mgr. for college periodical, member Drama Club.
Service:	Air Force Aviation Cadet Program University of Maryland Overseas Unit Course in Personnel Mgmt.

PERSONAL

Born:	1/15/38 in Brewer, ME. Height 6′2″; wt. 195.
Married:	5 children, self supporting.
Health:	Good; no physical limitations. Last physical - 1979.
Residence:	Rents home; free to relocate.
Hobbies:	Photography; amateur radio operator.

(FOR AMPLIFICATION PLEASE SEE FOLLOWING)
Pointing up qualities essential in all sales management: success in personal sales, coupled with success in getting maximum sales effort when managing salesmen.

Amplified Resume   Dudley M. Howard

EMPLOYMENT HIGHLIGHTS

8/79–Present

Appraiser and salesman. Immediately sought and found position, not in line with his experience and ability, but accepted on a temporary basis in preference to depriving family of income while seeking more suitable post. Present employer aware of circumstances, and may be contacted.

1976–8/79
MANSFIELD MOTORS

Employed as the second of four salesmen to revitalize sales in an agency in need of improved methods and sales. Sales rose substantially in first year; was appointed Sales Manager.

In this capacity, hired and trained 2 new salesmen in 1977, 3 more in 1978. Set up a realistic sales program; instituted a bonus system to stimulate sales activity. In addition, established a follow-up program for his men which operated as follows: each salesman was required to call on each car purchaser one week after sale. He was charged with the responsibility of checking on customer satisfaction, as well as to obtain names of friends who may have seen or ridden in the car, and could be logical prospects. A report on this call was mandatory, and proved valuable sales builder.

All sales promotions, administration and advertising came under his direction. Designed advertisements for local papers; developed special promotions. Among the unique promotions he conceived were "Old Timers Parties." Special invitations were issued former customers (now on inactive list), special new car showing program arranged, refreshments served; results were excellent.

Results:

As Salesman:
   Increased sales by 30% first year.

As Sales Manager:
   Showed increases of over 35% each year. Increase from 14 cars per month in '76, to 50 in 1978. Agency rose from 9th to 3rd in sales in the county.

Reason for leaving: Friction developed between partner-owners, resulting in sale of interest to outsider who moved in new sales staff. Resigned in protest of what he felt to be unreasonable discharge of competent sales personnel.

(continued)

Amplified Resume   Dudley M. Howard

1972–1976
RUTLAND MOTOR SALES

Employed as one of 15 salesmen. In approximately 2 years sales were in top 4 of the 15 salesmen; in 1976 was number one in sales. Resigned to accept offer above which had prospect of Sales Management.

1968–1972
VALLEY FORD, INC.

Employed as mechanic. In 4 months promoted to Service Foreman charged with general responsibility of analyzing car troubles for customer, writing up repair orders, maintain and build customer good will.

In approximately one year promoted to Service Manager, supervising the entire service operation (15 mechanics).

Reason for leaving: Resigned to go into sales.

1959–1968
LAKEPORT MARINE COMPANY

Employed as salesman on straight commission basis. Sales were such as to give him unusually good income for a strictly seasonal business.

Reason for leaving: Desired to get into business with more year-round potential.

REFERENCES

Available

Synopsis of Resume of:
RUSSEL R. HARRIS

25 Pickwick Dr.
Columbus, OH 43228
Phone: (614) 397-7762

JOB OBJECTIVE

Media Representative - any medium. Prefer newspaper or magazine.

EMPLOYMENT

1973-12/79	**ASSISTANT TO NATIONAL ADVERTISING MANAGER** Blaketon Newspapers Inc., Columbus, OH
1971-1973	**SALES PROMOTION** Warren Jam Kitchens Inc., Warren, OH

EDUCATION

1958-1961   Tilton Preparatory School, Tilton, NH
1962-1966   Williams College, Williamstown,MA
       Degree: B.A. Major: Economics
       Activities: Publicity Manager for Radio Station
         and College Theater Group; intramural sports; social fraternity.
1966-1968   Cornell University, Ithaca, NY
       Horticultural Course. Received diploma.

SERVICE

1968-1970   USAF
Facsimile Flight Supervisor, Andrews AFB, MD.
Maintained carrier and facsimile equipment in
Wash. D.C. area; placed in charge of Facsimile
Maint. Section at U.S. Weather Bureau, Suitland,
MD. last 6 months. Equipment transmitted weather
maps to 600 airports and bases throughout U.S.

PERSONAL

Born:	6/26/46 in Boston, MA. Height 5'10"; wt. 175
Married:	Wife graduate Mt. Holyoke College; one son.
Health:	Good; no physical limitations; last physical - 1979.
Residence:	Owns home and summer home.
Hobbies:	Swimming; Tennis; Golf.
Affiliations:	Radio and TV Executives Society; Board of Directors of Association of Commerce; National Executives Club; Rotary; Kiwanis; Chamber of Commerce.

(FOR AMPLIFICATION SEE FOLLOWING)
Showing specifics where possible (facts and figures) to establish scope of promotion effort in a broad, general field.

EMPLOYMENT HIGHLIGHTS

1973–12/79
BLAKETON NEWSPAPERS INC.

Originally employed as advertising salesman assigned to small business firms.

After one year promoted, with salary raise, to department store contact. Work involved multiple contacts on each account: advertising departments, buyers, and the advertising agency representing each account. Required blending all ideas into a successful sale, insuring desirable, available space, while maintaining volume advertising from company's largest customers.

Advanced with new salary increase to "Special Promotions". Included were plaza openings, Civic Memorial dedication, and similar large events. Introduced change from former procedure of burdening only the builders, contractors and suppliers for advertising. Advertising from the owner or operator was added. Innovation resulted in far greater promotional return. In developing such a promotion, was in competition with two equally large daily newspapers. However, was consistently successful in developing 20 to 25 page section, with an advertising take in five figures. Was required to sell idea to all advertisers (up to 60 in one promotion), coordinate entire program.

1976 promoted to Assistant to National Advertising Manager for company's three newspapers. Duties were varied. Assumed full responsibility for national food advertising; contributed ideas for departmental reorganization; called on national advertisers throughout the state.

Results: 1. Through departmental streamlining cut staff by 3, while handling increased volume.
2. Company evaluation of services indicated by salary increase of $16,000 from start of employment.

Reason for change: Resigned to assist group who planned to purchase and publish a weekly newspaper. Plan abandoned on death of head of group.

1971–1973
WARREN JAM KITCHENS INC.

Introduced mail order sales, developed special holiday packaging, substantially broadening market and increasing sales volume. Stepped up newspaper advertising, added television and radio. Results were similar to those described above; resigned to accept position offered.

Excellent References Available

Synopsis of Resume of:
HAROLD J. BEALE

44 Holly Rd.
Salem, OR 97306
Phone: (503) 421–8753

JOB OBJECTIVE

Shop Supervision, Welding Foreman, Instructor in Welding.

EMPLOYMENT

1970–Present   SPECIALTY WELDER, WELDER FOREMAN
Cooper-Noonan Div. Salem Steel Inc.
Salem, OR

1969–1975   SELF-EMPLOYED - owner welding shop and welding school.
Operated days, while employed above at night. School operated at
request of Cooper-Noonan; closed 1975 due to lack of materials.

Prior   Farm work during high school period.

EDUCATION

Wolf Point High School, Wolf Point, MT
Graduated.
Makey Welding School, Boise, ID. 1968.
One year welding course, incldued acetylene welding.
Other:
I.C.S. Welding Course, varied safety, and
miscellaneous company courses.

PERSONAL

Born: 1/5/42 in Wolf Point, MT. Height 5'8"; wt. 175 lbs.
Married: Widower; one son self-supporting.
Health: Good; no physical limitations.
Hobbies: Restoring antique cars; camping.
Civic: Active in sundry civic and church fund raising drives, has been
chairman of several.

(FOR AMPLIFICATION PLEASE SEE FOLLOWING)
*Level of supervisory responsibility shown through number of persons supervised; success of effort shown
through promotion.*

Amplified Resume   Harold J. Beale

EMPLOYMENT

1970–Present
COOPER-NOONAN - Div. Salem Steel Inc.

Originally employed in Template Shop as helper, moved to multiple punch helper to welder.

Promoted to Welding Inspector; served as sole plant inspector to 320 welders.

Promoted to Foreman (approximately 50 welders) in Marine Division of Salem Steel.

Appointed Navy Yard Instructor for new welders. Note: was also training welders in own shop and school at request of the company. Total working hours: approximately 15 hrs. per day, 7 days per week.

Appointed welding Foreman on Navy Yard Outfitting Docks. Employed in this capacity until returning to plant as Specialty Welder when navy work slowed down (1978).

Continues to serve as Specialty and Acetylene welder, considered to be plant's specialist or expert welder. Collaborates with engineering department in tests of new varieties of welding materials; assists in making decisions on recommended changes.

Reason for desiring change: Feels future prospects in steel industry uncertain. Would make change anywhere (including overseas) for connection with progressive company fully utilizing his extensive experience.

REFERENCES

Personal references available on request.
Please no contact with present company until after interview.

Synopsis of Resume of:
LINDA ROTH

3 Woodthrush Drive
West Nyack, NY 10994
Phone: (914) 358-7917

JOB OBJECTIVE

Position as social worker emphasizing individual contacts within a therapeutic community.

EDUCATION

Fordham University, Graduate School of Social Service
at Lincoln Center, NY
M.S.W., June 1975.
Major: Services to Individuals and Families
Minor: Services to Groups

St. Thomas Aquinas College, Sparkill, NY
B.A., June 1971. Cum Laude.
Major: English
Minor: Education

Rockland Community College, Suffern, N.Y.
A.A., June 1966. Cum Laude.

EXPERIENCE

1974-1975   ROCKLAND COUNTY COMMUNITY MENTAL HEALTH
CENTER
Pomona, NY.
Field Placement.

1975-Present VOLUNTEER COUNSELING SERVICE
151 S. Main St., New York, NY.
Field Placement, Counselor, Supervisor

PERSONAL

Born: June 3, 1930. Height 5'5"; wt. 130.
Married: 3 children: 23, 21, 18.
Health: Excellent, no physical limitations.
Hobbies: Tennis, swimming, handicrafts.
Affiliations: National Association of Social Workers, Member Association for
Retarded Children

(FOR AMPLIFICATION PLEASE SEE FOLLOWING)
*Mature woman entering field at professional level after completing family responsibilities. Excellent
education and field experience stressed in place of work experience in non-related areas.*

Amplified Resume   Linda Roth

1974–1975
ROCKLAND COUNTY COMMUNITY MENTAL HEALTH CENTER

Responsibilities included crisis intervention and short term and long term treatment of patients (adolescents and adults) with a full range of diagnostic categories and wide socioeconomic backgrounds.

Co-therapist in weekly crisis intervention group with a variety of intrapsychic and interpersonal problems. Emergency suicide and hospitalization evaluations intake; diagnostic assessment. Consultations with psychiatrists and community agencies. Familiarity with medications.

Supervisor: Jane Driscoll, M.S.W., Acting Director, Emergency Service and Admissions.

1975–Present
VOLUNTEER COUNSELING SERVICE

Individual, marital, and family counseling with referrals from Family Court, Probation Department, and community agencies. Responsibilities included intake-diagnostic assessment, screening new volunteer counselors, training new counselors, administration, community organization, and public relations for fund raising.

Supervisor: John Schamus, A.C.S.W., Assistant Director.

REFERENCES

Available upon request.

Resume of:
STANISLAUS KOWALSKI

87 Hills St.
Amherst, MA 01002
Phone: (617) 643–9840

JOB OBJECTIVE

Language instructor at college level. Desires location which would permit continued study.

CHRONOLOGY

8/68–Present	UNIVERSITY OF MASS., Amherst, MA U.S. Air Force Institute of Technology Div. Teacher of Russian and Polish languages.
1963–6/68	Sundry factory employments to repay large indebtedness. (See amplification for detail).

1960–1963	TOLSTOY FOUNDATION, New York, NY
	  Met and assisted incoming refugees; involved
	  clerical work, typing, translation, etc.

1957–1960	UNRRA and IRO in French Zone of Occupation. Interpreter, translator, direction of refugees.
1956–1957	FRENCH MILITARY GOV'T. French Zone of Occupation, South Germany Interpreter.
Prior	Foreign language lessons and tutoring during college period.

EDUCATION

College:	French School of Languages, Warsaw, Poland. Specialized in: French, German, Polish, Russian. University of Warsaw: Russian language and literature.

Miscellaneous:	Has studied Spanish language by self teaching method.
	Credited by U. of Mass. with 2 year's college credit
	from records salvaged to date; attempting to locate
	additional records. Familiar with following languages:
	  Russian, Polish, French, German, Spanish, English,
	  Czech, Bulgarian and Serbo-Croatian.

PERSONAL

Born:	3/10/31 in Warsaw, Poland. Height 5'10"; wt. 175 lbs.
Marital status:	Widower. Citizenship: application filed.
Health:	Excellent; no physical limitations. Last physical 1979.

(FOR AMPLIFICATION PLEASE SEE FOLLOWING)
*Teaching/language aspect of record is emphasized in order to account for constructive and
directed effort during intermittent years.*

Amplified Resume   Stanislaus Kowalski

Highlights of U.S. Employment

8/68–Present
UNIVERSITY OF MASS.

Employed as Russian and Polish language instructor for Air Force personnel. Conducts 5 to 6 classes per day with a total of 6 teaching hours daily 6 days per week on a 12 month per year program.

Results have been excellent; class attendance well above average; student interest high. University has rewarded him with 4 salary increases; has retained him while reducing staff.

Responsibilities assumed include tape recorded lessons and lesson plan preparation. Also corrected text material prepared by school due to lack of good text books.

Reason for desiring change: Position which would permit more time to pursue his education and obtain degree.

GENERAL

Formal education terminated with outbreak of war. Remained in Poland; put in work camp. Escaped, remained near Swiss border of Germany until French took over that sector. Employment with French Military Government and UNRRA (listed on synopsis page) followed.

Father had been on staff of American Embassy in Warsaw; friends in U.S. State Department aided family in entering United States in 1960.

Employment with Tolstoy Foundation followed (see synopsis); terminated when it became necessary to seek sundry factory employments to repay large indebtedness incurred during prolonged illness and ultimate death of father. With debt load cleared in 1968, returned to educational field.

REFERENCES

Available from U.S. Employers

Synopsis of Resume of:
THOMAS R. COLE

76 Hollister Rd.
Orlando, FL 32815
Phone: (305) 928–6301

JOB OBJECTIVE

Position in Field of Technical Writing

EMPLOYMENT

9/69–Present and 1965–1967	**TECHNICAL WRITER** Florida Electronics Corp., Orlando, FL
10/68–8/69	**TECHNICIAN** Capital Electric Co., Jacksonville, FL
4/63–1964	**FIELD ENGINEER** (U.S. and Germany) Krylex Corporation, New York, NY

EDUCATION

College:	Orlando Technical Institute, Orlando, FL Attends classes 3 nights per week; Graduated with A.A.S. in Electrical Engineering 6/73
Misc:	Hung Radio Engineering School (correspondence) Hytron Transistor Course
Languages:	French and Italian (limited); German (fluent).

SERVICE

1961–2/63	U.S. Army Attended Radio Mechanics School; served as radio technician in Germany. Language proficiency resulted in transfer to personnel office; worked with German employees on base; taught German language to group of service men.

PERSONAL

Born:	10/9/40 in Winona, MN. Height 5′8″; wt. 160 lbs.
Married:	2 self-supporting children.
Health:	Good; no physical limitations; last complete physical 12/79.
Residence:	Rents home; free to relocate.
Hobbies:	Water sports; sailing; stamp collecting.

(FOR AMPLIFICATION SEE FOLLOWING)

Broken employment presented in chronological, one-employment form for clarity. To increase resume circulation potential, change of area as "Reason for Leaving" normally avoided. It is used only on the premise that prospective employer in a given area could be favorably influenced by employee preference for that area.

Amplified Resume   Thomas R. Cole

EMPLOYMENT HIGHLIGHTS

1965–Present (except for interval below)
FLORIDA ELECTRONICS CORP.

'65   Employed as tester and trouble shooter on electronic equipment. Took specimens
           from line production, gave them rigid tests. If trouble developed, located source.

'66   Promoted to Laboratory Technician. Performed simulated environmental tests
           (temperature, humidity, acceleration, shock, etc.) on components and electrical
           circuits. Also wrote engineering reports based on data compiled. These compre-
           hensive reports formed basis for the expenditure of several thousands of dollars
           of company funds.

'67   Promoted to Senior Laboratory Technician, assigned to development testing of
           transistorized switching and pulse circuitry. Wrote engineering reports on find-
           ings.

10/68   Left to accept better paying position below.

9/69   Rehired as Technical Writer with substantial salary increase. Work is on the
           upper level of theoretical operation of electronic devices, as compared to "Manual
           of Operation" writer. Devices described are highly complex, with manuals written
           in the language of circuitry, taken from the logic form of circuit schematics.
           Manuals are for use by technicians.

           Familiar with government and commercial specifications on the writing of both
           operation and theory manuals. Has written material dealing with solid-state,
           computer, and electronic switching circuitry. Is capable of writing and editing
           own material as well as supervising production of final copy from start to finish.

           Reason for desiring change: To relocate in the North.

10/68–9/69
CAPITAL ELECTRIC COMPANY

    Employed as technician. Made responsible for testing and development of permanent
    magnet generators, plus maintenance of test equipment.

    Was successful in correcting variety of improper procedures and faults in construction
    with resultant company savings.

    Reason for leaving: To accept technical writing position and substantial pay increase
    offered by former employer.

(continued)

Amplified Resume

4/63–1964
KRYLEX CORPORATION (Automatic fire control systems)

Following service, employed as Field Engineer of Baltimore, MD. division, engaged in the maintenance and modification of the K-99 automatic control fire system (a radar and computer controlled anti-aircraft gun).

Served as company representative at military installation in Hamburg, Germany. Inspected equipment, made changes where required.

Reason for change: To return to U.S. for marriage.

REFERENCES

Available on request

Synopsis of Resume of:
ALAN ENNIS

408 Sabrina Lane
Dallas, TX 75218
Phone: (214) 942–2609

JOB OBJECTIVE

Staff Weatherman

EMPLOYMENT

1977–Present	WQXY-TV, Dallas, TX Weather Service Director
1976–1977	WLS-TV, Chicago, IL Staff weather forecaster
1974–1976	WIVI-FM, St. Croix, U.S. Virgin Islands Staff Announcer Newsman Promotions Manager
1972–1974	WBMD-AM-FM, Bradenton, FL Staff announcer; disc jockey.

EDUCATION

1969–1972	University of Texas, Austin, TX Emphasis: Radio, TV, Film.
1968	Bryan Junior College, Dallas, TX Emphasis: Speech, announcing techniques.

PERSONAL

Born:	1949, in Slidell, MS. Marital status: single.
Health:	Excellent; no physical limitations.
Appearance:	Height 5'11"; weight 154.
Hobbies:	Flying (have private license); sports car rallying; music.
Affiliations:	American Meteorological Society.

(FOR AMPLIFICATION PLEASE SEE FOLLOWING)

Amplified Resume

Page 2
Allen Ennis

1977–Present

Employed as staff announcer and promotions manager of WQXY-TV in Dallas, Texas. In addition to standard staff announcing and promotional work, assisted in production of local shows and commercials. Selected as temporary replacement for weatherman after approximately six months. After a three-week trial period, was offered and accepted the permanent post with salary increase. While in the position, constructed an APT (weather satellite) ground station to receive and track major satellites; developed a system to display national weather service radar on a character generator.

Reason for leaving: New management requires weatherman position be filled with person having degree in meteorology.

1976–1977

Employed by the American Broadcasting Co., WLS-TV in Chicago, IL, as weather forecaster for weekend news show. Duties included assisting in preparing weekday weather shows, plus preparing script and voice-over for weather stories fed on DEF news feed.

Reason for leaving: Cancellation of three weekend news shows.

1974–1976

Employed as staff announcer, promotions manager, and newsman by WIVI-TV in the Virgin Islands. Limited staff resulted in fulfilling many additional responsibilities, including formating and participation in all night weekend variety shows. No ratings available.

Reason for leaving: Desire to return to the states and greater opportunity.

1972–1974

Worked on volunteer basis for WBMD radio in Bradenton, FL after college. When opening occurred, was hired at nominal salary for general duties. Selected as vacation replacement for currently popular deejay. Format: strict MOR. Raised show rating to number one (ratings by Mediastat); consequently, was given show as permanent assignment. Kept show in number one rating spot until voluntary resignation to accept position in the Virgin Islands.

Summary

Experienced in all phases of radio and television, but find strongest interest in the field of weather. Anticipate working toward degree in meteorology if such an arrangement is feasible and satisfactory with prospective employer.

REFERENCES

On Request

Synopsis of Resume of:
GERALD L. MAURER

76 Caldwell St.
Binghamton, NY 13903
Phone: (716) 643–3419

JOB OBJECTIVE

Position as Tool Engineer or related activity

EMPLOYMENT

1/76–Present	**TOOL ENGINEER** Ansco, Binghamton, NY (1500 employees. Producers of: color photographic film, microfilm, copy papers, etc.)
1961–12/75	FOREMAN (tool and die group) - moved up from apprentice. Marx Tool & Gauge Co., Trenton, NJ (Largest shop of kind east of Mississippi).

EDUCATION

1959	East High School, Allentown, PA Graduate. President of class Jr. year.
1961–1964	Tool and Die Making Apprenticeship. Completed all courses including blueprint reading.
Misc:	Moderate knowledge of German; excellent command of English.
General:	Financed brother's business college education.

SERVICE

10/59–2/61	U.S. Air Force. Private to Airman 2/c. Served in U.S. and Germany. Hon. Discharge; no reserve obligation.

PERSONAL

Born:	7/2/41 in Allentown, PA. Married, 2 children.
Appearance:	Height 5′11″; wt. 175 lbs. Health: excellent.
Residence:	Owns home; willing to relocate.
Hobbies:	Baseball (Capt. softball team); bowling; camping.
Affiliations:	American Legion; church member.

(FOR AMPLIFICATION PLEASE SEE FOLLOWING)

Despite lack of formal training, applicant demonstrates high degree of self-development, as shown by level of responsibility and concrete dollar-and-cents results. Reason for leaving could not be briefly stated; is best omitted, to be discussed at interview.

Amplified Resume   Gerald L. Maurer

EMPLOYMENT HIGHLIGHTS

1/76–Present
ANSCO

Employed as Tool Engineer with responsibilities that included the following:

Direction of machine shop.

Determination of equipment required to handle foreseeable production.

Development of cost of necessary equipment, practicability of production within company or farming to outside vendors.

Assistance in preparation of drawings and data necessary for producing equipment within or without the plant.

Cooperation with Quality Control in solution of problems connected with production machinery.

Improvement of existing production machinery to improve product or production, reduce maintenance or down time.

Results:

1. Determined cause of rapid wear of German made dies for punching track in film. Improved die life from 6 weeks to 11 months. As costly dies required 10 to 12 months for delivery, also resulted in substantial savings in inventory.

2. Improved operation of film and paper backing slitting machines entirely eliminating a loss of 3 cuts in every 30, and a second loss of 4 in 12 on second coating of same film, thereby compounding the savings on tens of thousands of film rolls daily.

3. Eliminated costly die purchase by creation of fixture to make deckel edge dies in company shop.

4. Conceived idea of recutting to smaller standard size film which was formerly discarded for improper slitting. Supervised rework of machine (formerly used for different purpose). Savings have exceeded $2,500 monthly.

5. Revamped inoperative machines; accomplished major rejuvenation of production machines.

Reason for desiring change: To be discussed at interview.

(continued)

Amplified Resume   Gerald L. Maurer

1961–12/75
MARX TOOL & GAUGE CO.
(Company was one of top concerns in U.S. doing machine shop and tooling work for major companies such as: GM, GE, Bethlehem Steel, etc.)

Following apprenticeship, had unusual opportunity of working with and under direction of expert diemaker, who, as an experienced perfectionist, gave him a 6 year post-graduate course in tool and die work.

Spent one year in estimating and related work, then promoted to Foreman of Die Makers. In this capacity headed group of 10 older, more experienced men. Despite lack of seniority, encountered no personnel problems. Was given work which could not be produced in company shops (including major companies shown above). Some work engineered by clients, some by Marx, some by both. Achieved outstanding record of no work returned for reworking, no failures.

Dies produced were for such miscellaneous uses as: mold dies for Bethlehem Steel, key dies for IBM, die to produce (in one stamping) the entire dashboard for Imperial Brougham - die wt. 16,000 lbs.

Regularly visited customer plants where dies were delivered to insure proper use, correct temperatures, etc. This involved extensive travel to eastern and middle eastern U.S. Was also called on for trouble shooting customer equipment not necessarily produced by Marx, and involved machines not limited to die work.

Reason for leaving: Employment terminated when company closed.

REFERENCES

Available on Request

Synopsis of Resume of:
NICHOLAS A. ROCHE

78 Doyle St.
Trenton, NJ 08607
Phone: (609) 242−9003

JOB OBJECTIVE

Position as Traffic Manager or Assistant

EMPLOYMENT

7/66–Present   ELECTRONIC DIV. OF WESTINGHOUSE INC., Trenton, NJ
Yearly income has increased by $10,500 since 1966.
Senior rate clerk.

2/60–6/66   ALLIED TRANSPORT COMPANY, Perth Amboy, NJ
Assistant Terminal Manager.

EDUCATION

Carver High School, St. Paul, MN
    Graduated 1954.
Service Courses included:
    Electrical Theory; Mathematics.
Traffic Managers Institute, Perth Amboy, NJ
    Course in ICC Law and Procedure.
Braden Institute, Trenton, NJ. Night School.
    Course in Traffic Management. Graduated 1st in class.

PERSONAL

Born: 12/5/36 in St. Paul, MN. Height 6′1″; wt. 165 lbs.
              Married, 3 children.
Health: Good; no physical limitations.
Residence: Rents home; free to relocate.
Hobbies: Do-it-yourself home projects; spectator sports.
Affiliations: Transportation Club of Trenton.
Civic: Former Vice Pres. of Little Leagues of Perth Amboy, NJ.

(FOR AMPLIFICATION PLEASE SEE FOLLOWING)
*Long-term employment amplified in chronological detail to point up positive progression not fully reflected
by position title.*

Amplified Resume   Nicholas Roche

EMPLOYMENT

7/66–Present
ELECTRONIC DIVISION OF WESTINGHOUSE INC.

1966
Employed as Junior Rate Clerk; processed and audited freight bills, traced shipments. After 4 months was put in charge of scheduling shipments from new warehouse at distance from plant. Ordered and scheduled trucks, routed shipments, set up operations which he turned over to regular shipping group. Accomplished in less than 2 months.

1967
Promoted to Senior Rate Clerk. Actually assumed duties of Traffic Manager, as title holder was made Purchasing Agent and spent full time in that function. Had complete supervision over personnel, gave assignments, made contacts with transportation companies, routed shipments, etc. During this period devised routing charts, revamped filing system, set up rate charts, leveled distribution so equitably among carriers that exceptional shipping service was obtained.

1976
On return of aforementioned Traffic Manager to department, was given salary raise and unofficial title of Assistant Traffic Manager; formal classification remained Senior Rate Clerk. Handles all technical matters within the department; attends meetings of the Traffic and Rate Committee (nationwide). Is familiar with all procedures, regulations, laws and tariffs; does some import and export work.

Special Assignments:
    Has been sent by company to Phoenix, Arizona, and Sacramento, California to select distribution warehouses. Selection approved.
    Has charge of movement of 79 specially equipped rail cars assigned to company; watches their travel and insures return for loading.

Savings: As a result of his efforts, company has used intercoastal shipping instead of rail. Has shown 40% savings on sizeable electronic component shipments.

Reason for desiring change: Position fully utilizing on-the-job experience and training as well as recently completed advanced traffic mgmt. course.

2/58–6/76
ALLIED TRANSPORT CO.

Employed as manifest clerk; promoted to Rate & Billing Clerk, to Office Mgr. supervising previous work and clerks. Transferred to Trenton as Assistant Terminal Mgr. Left to accept better position above.

References Available

3

For Women Returning To The Job Market

Displaced Homemakers

Not too many years ago, when a woman who was "just a housewife" was widowed, divorced or separated, she was left alone to fend for herself. Now, such a woman has been raised to the status of "Displaced Homemaker" and is receiving support services from local Displaced Homemaker Re-Entry Programs.

According to Laurie Shields, a co-founder of the Displaced Homemaker Movement, there are an estimated 189,000 displaced homemakers in New England alone. This indicates a national figure that is quite substantial.

The official definition of a displaced homemaker is a person (usually over 35) who has worked in the home providing unpaid services for a family for a number of years, and is forced suddenly into the labor market.

Although the removal of age discrimination barriers are a pragmatic solution to the older person's job hunt, it's realistic to acknowledge that certain psychological barriers remain. It's up to the erstwhile "housewife" to hammer away at the image until it is changed, and it's gradually happening. The motivation is sheer survival—and it's a strong one.

Look for a Displaced Homemakers Program in your area. If none is available, call local high schools for adult education course listings. They often include peer group rap sessions with titles such as "Widow to Widow Lift" or "Divorce, A New Beginning."

An alternative is to take a refresher course in an old skill: typing, bookkeeping, sewing, home decorating, cake decorating, flower arranging, creative writing.

Make use of your transferable skills. Restaurants and tea rooms use good cooking and baking skills. Florists use flower arranging skills. Stores use sales persons knowledgeable in childrens' clothing, housewares and home decorating.

Displaced homemakers may need their confidence bolstered. A volunteer job is a good start. It provides needed structure in grooming, being some place on time at definite hours, mixing with strangers, and a sense of self-worth.

The paying job for the displaced homemaker reentering the labor market is often at the entry-level, a fact of life acknowledged by the Labor Department. However, the sky's the limit once she's in, and a proper resume can immeasureably aid the entry.

This section of the book contains sample resumes of displaced homemakers with various degrees of skills and experience, as well as varied goals.

Synopsis of Resume of:
MARILYN NEAL CULLEN

9876 Venice Blvd.
Culver City, CA 90034
Phone: (213) 352–9007

OBJECTIVE

Position with potential requiring good verbal and writing skills; advertising, copy writing. Would consider sales with potential.

EXPERIENCE

1980–Present   SALES
                  Mail order sportswear sold through party plan.

1969–1980   FREE LANCE WRITING
                  Part-time while raising family.

1968   DRESS SHOP MANAGER
                  "Mary Del Shop" women's apparel.

Prior   Before marriage was Assistant Fashion Coordinator, and Assistant to Advertising Director for shoe company.

EDUCATION

College: Nassau Community College
                      Major: English Literature

Other: Betty Owen Secretarial Systems
                      Shorthand 100 WPM; Typing 60 WPM.
                   George Mercer School of Theology.
                      Degree in Religious Education.

PERSONAL

Born: 1929; married, 4 children, 2 self-supporting. Health - good.
Hobbies: Music; sewing; sketching; writing.
Affiliations: Member church choir; Literary Club.

(FOR AMPLIFICATION SEE FOLLOWING)

Recently divorced—dislikes word; consequently not used so she may be comfortable with her resume at this initial contact stage. Sales picked from record to focus on qualifications for objective.

Amplified Resume   Marilyn Neal Cullen - page 2

EXPERIENCE HIGHLIGHTS

**1980–Present
SALES**

Interim work while seeking full-time career objective. Sells line of women's sportswear through home party plan. Makes own contacts, sets up appointments, models and shows line. Takes orders and follows through to delivery and customer satisfaction. Increased sales to point has hired an assistant.

**1969–1980
FREE-LANCE WRITING**

During years of marriage and raising family worked from home doing free-lance writing assignments. Included writing and editing travel guide for "Association of Informed Travelers," a series of articles on an experimental educational project, and radio copy.

During this period did church related volunteer work. Appointed Prayer Chairman responsible for opening and closing board meetings as well as luncheon invocations, was promoted to General Chairman. In this capacity multiple functions included: chairing 20-member board meetings, coordinating public luncheon meetings for up to 140 persons.

**1968
MANAGEMENT**

As Manager for women's apparel shop, "Mary Del," hired and supervised sales personnel, scheduled floor time, and assisted in closing sales. Did all bookkeeping and banking. Left due to pregnancy.

Prior

Following college, employed by Chas. Stevens Co. of St. Louis in Lingerie Dept. Promoted to manager of department, supervised full and part-time employees, gained experience in all aspects, including inventory.

Filled in as model for in-store fashion shows, given additional responsibility as Assistant Fashion Coordinator. Named member of "Shoe Fashion Board of St. Louis," one of five women who met monthly formulating articles and giving interviews to local news media on fashion trends in shoe industry. Designed and modeled shoes; acted as liaison between factory and store.
Left for marriage.

REFERENCES

Available

Synopsis of Resume of:
ELEANOR OWEN

875 Sparkman Blvd.
Tucson, AZ 85716
Phone: (602) 884–9633

JOB OBJECTIVE

Executive Director, preferably with non-profit organization.

EXPERIENCE

1978–Present	DISPLACED HOMEMAKER SERVICE, Tucson, Arizona 440 Lincoln Blvd. Director.
1976–1978	HOME CARE CORPS FOR SENIOR CITIZENS Pittsburgh, Pennsylvania. Supervisor.
1972–1976	COMMUNITY ADVOCATE, JOB DEVELOPER Boston, Mass.
1966–1972	CHARLES STONE ASSOCIATES Boston, Mass. Economist.
1965	NYS DEPT. OF LABOR Rome, New York Labor Market Analyst.
1960–1965	CHAMBER OF COMMERCE Oak Ridge, Tenn. Manager
Prior	Public School Teacher

EDUCATION

B.A.	Boston University - Economics, Business Administration.
M.S.	Brooklyn College - Economic Development & Education.
Other:	Special courses in: Administration of Voluntary Civic Organizations; Job Analysis; Administration and Planning of Social Service Delivery Programs; Evaluation of Social Security Development Programs; Supervision in a Social Service Agency.

PERSONAL

Mature, in good health, owns and drives car, free to travel or relocate.

(FOR AMPLIFICATION SEE FOLLOWING)
Older woman in specialized field who can literally "stand on her record," which is highlighted. Personal details kept to minimum, and all positive.

Amplified Resume

Eleanor Owen - Page 2

EXPERIENCE

1978–Present
DISPLACED HOMEMAKER SERVICES

Director of state-funded program. Plans and supervises program, including training, counseling, liaison with community resources, outreach and public relations. Feels degree of authority assured has been fragmented; would make change for similar position with full reign.

1976–1978
HOME CARE CORPS FOR SENIOR CITIZENS

Supervised staff of 30. Directed eight programs funded under Title III of the Older Americans Act, including Shuttle Service, Income Maintenance, Housing Advocacy, and Visiting Aides. Planned, supervised housing outreach program. Interviewed 78% of the target population; supervised preparation of submitted report. Left for new challenge above.

1972–1976
COMMUNITY ADVOCATE

In this project "Retain," responsibilities included outreach, public relations, volunteer supervision, intake interviews, job placement and development. Goal: to change attitude of business community towards the employment of the older job seeker in private industry. Project satisfactorily completed.

1966–1972
CHARLES STONE ASSOCIATES

Researched and developed criteria for public facilities grants to localities to alleviate long-term unemployment. Wrote proposals on cost/benefit criteria for "Safety On The Highway" grants.

1965
NYS DEPT. OF LABOR

Employed on special project as labor market analyst to explore employment status of displaced Sperry Rand employees several months after company moved to another area. Results showed direct correlation between the employee's age and present employment status.

1960–1965
CHAMBER OF COMMERCE

Supervised budget, community relations, membership drives and chamber's multiple committees. Planned and wrote an economic analysis of region. Organized Tourist Bureau. Increased membership by 20%, tourist inquiries by 50%. Left for lower pressure project above.

REFERENCES ON REQUEST

Synopsis of Resume of:
REGINA T. BRODY

29 South St.
Minneapolis, MN 55401
Phone: (612) 333-1989

JOB OBJECTIVE

Editing, Writing, Research. Free to travel on own or as assistant.

Present
RESEARCH ASSISTANT. Assistant to author of book on American Art Museums. Part-time work on hourly pay scale.

1972-1980
VOLUNTEER WORK. Director Parent-Child Day Care Center. Teacher's aide and tutor in public schools.

1965-1972
DEMONSTRATION SCHOOL OF NATIONAL COLLEGE OF EDUCATION.
Teacher

1961-1965
WIEBOLDT FOUNDATION FUNDED PROJECT.
Science Consultant and Assistant.

EDUCATION

B.A.   Wellesley College, Wellesley, Mass.
M.Ed.   Nat. College of Education, Evanston, Ill.

PUBLICATIONS

Young People's Science Encyclopedia - Science Editor.
Science Activities From A to Z - co-author.
Value Sharing: Creative Strategy - co-author.

PERSONAL

Born: 1927; recent widow; 3 self-supporting children.
Health: Excellent. Height 5'6"; wt. 117 lbs.
Hobbies: Tennis; golf; travel; theater; music.
Affiliations: Wellesley Club; American Pen Women's Club.

(FOR AMPLIFICATION PLEASE SEE NEXT PAGE)
Analysis: Well-educated, trim, active woman, gleaned from personal and education data. Has substantial private income, subtly indicated by job objective, and expertise to back up goal documented by listed "publications".

Amplified Resume   Regina T. Brody - page 2

EXPERIENCE HIGHLIGHTS

Present
RESEARCH ASSISTANT

Recommended by local art gallery to author researching book on American Museums; edited his work, as well as doing additional research on own. Also has written short biographical sketches of selected artists. Project scheduled for completion late 1980. Hourly wage doubled since work began; excellent letter of reference available.

1972–1980
VOLUNTEER WORK

As wife of successful banker in no need of income, became actively engaged in community projects on volunteer basis. Assisted in fund raising drive to establish a Parent-Child Day Care Center, and served as its director for four years. Full-time five day week responsibilities. Acted as teacher's aide and science tutor at both junior high and elementary public school level.

1965–1972
DEMONSTRATION SCHOOL OF NATIONAL COLLEGE OF EDUCATION

In addition to teaching 6th grade, was responsible for supervision of student teachers. Did demonstration lessons for closed-circuit television, lecturing to students enrolled in the various college courses. Required careful course preparation as well as interesting presentation to sustain viewer interest. Supervised student participation in the program. Resigned when husband was transferred from area.

1961–1965
RESEARCH PROJECT

Employed as Science Consultant and Assistant to administrator of research project funded by Wieboldt Foundation in Chicago. Project structured around a social-psychological framework developed by Harold Lasswell of Yale. Staffed by National College of Education and administered in five Chicago schools (K through 8). Edited final report.

REFERENCES

On request. Copies of publications available for review.

Synopsis of Resume of:
JANET PIERCE

59 E. Connor St.
Sheridan, WY 82801
Phone: (307) 324–4760

JOB OBJECTIVE

Free-lance writing

EDUCATION

College   Milwaukee-Downer College, Milwaukee, Wisconsin
B.A. Major: English Lit.

University of Michigan.
Graduate work, teacher's certificate courses.

Findlay College, Findlay, Ohio.
Business courses. Typing, shorthand, dictaphone.

Columbia University.
Journalism Workshop.

Other: Languages.
Fluent Spanish; working knowledge of French.

EMPLOYMENT

1975–Present   Shopping Guide Inc., Sheridan, Wyoming.
Food columnist.

Prior   Oakland Press, Pontiac, Michigan.
Women's Editor. Promoted from part-time food writer.

Pontiac Michigan Board of Education.
Taught speech and creative writing adult ed. classes.

PERSONAL

Born: 1915; married, excellent health, 5'2", high energy.
Hobbies: Reading; jogging; cooking; crafts; theatre; music.
Affiliations: Member: AAUW, National Federation of Press Women. On board of
Friends of Arts and Sciences, and community theatre group.

(FOR AMPLIFICATION PLEASE SEE FOLLOWING)
*Mature woman endowed with "high energy" as indicated by eagerness to take continued education courses
and remain involved with or without pay.*

Amplified Resume   Janet Pierce - page 2

EMPLOYMENT HIGHLIGHTS

1975–Present
SHOPPING GUIDE INC. (weekly newspaper)

Following husband's retirement to Wyoming, approached paper with idea of writing a food column featuring various items advertised as "weekly specials" by food markets. Given trial period at no salary; however, idea proved so successful was hired as weekly columnist and given bonus for increased food advertising, which has resulted.

Reason for change: Required to be in newspaper office several days a week. Would like position working out of own home.

PRIOR

Oakland Press, Pontiac, Michigan.

Employed as part-time food writer. Steadily advanced to Food Editor, Home Editor and Feature Writer. During nearly twenty year tenure gained thorough knowledge of all newspaper aspects, including importance of meeting deadlines, dependability and professionalism.

Was promoted to Women's Editor, while continuing as Food Editor. Job terminated with sale of newspaper to Tri-Cities who brought in own staff.

Pontiac Board of Education

Simultaneous with above, volunteered to teach creative writing and speech classes for evening adult education classes. Three students moved on to successful, professional writing careers.

Girl Scouts of America

Filled in for Girl Scout Executive during 6 mos. temporary leave of absence. Is skilled in, and taught variety of, crafts.

REFERENCES

On Request

Synopsis of Resume of:
SALLY PETTIGREW

302 Liberty St.
Charleston, WV 25424
Phone: (304) 253–3471

CAREER OBJECTIVE

In Production Department of middle-sized publication, as apprentice or refresher trainee.
Hours flexible.

EXPERIENCE

1965–1972   PRODUCTION MANAGER. Started as typesetter.
Roanoke Gazette - weekly newspaper with over
15,000 circulation

1963–1964   LIBRARIAN
Chemical Abstracts, Columbus, Ohio.

1962–1963   RECREATIONAL THERAPIST, Columbus, Ohio
Ohio State School for Retarded

EDUCATION

1960–1962   Miami University, Oxford, Ohio.
Journalism major.

1957–1960   North High School, Columbus, Ohio.
Editor school paper and senior annual.

Other: Seminars on typography of newspapers.

Skills: Typewriter; Compugraphic I; Editwriter 7700.

Strengths: Spelling, grammar, organization, detail.

PERSONAL

Born: 1942; single, 2 dependent school-age children.
Health: Excellent; height 5′5″; wt. 125 lbs. Owns home and car.
Hobbies: Reading; writing; needle point; swimming.
Affiliations: Junior League; Secretary PTA.

(FOR AMPLIFICATION SEE FOLLOWING)

Recent divorcee who has assumed maiden name. Children mentioned as they will ultimately be a factor in determining job hours. Although she has not worked since 1972, it is not emphasized, though realistically recognized in wording of job objective.

Amplified Resume   Sally Pettigrew - page 2

CAREER HIGHLIGHTS

1965–1972
ROANOKE GAZETTE - 17 employees

Hired as typesetter on part-time basis filling in during vacations and sundry illness and pregnancy leaves-of-absence of primarily female staff.

As proficiency increased, was given assignments of longer duration and ultimately hired on full-time basis for typesetting and assisting in production department with layout. As paper circulation increased along with advertising, it was determined a larger staff was needed in production, and was moved full-time into that department.

In 1970 made Production Manager. In that capacity had overall charge of: (1) laying out entire paper, which ran from 24 to 48 pages depending on percentage of advertising; (2) advertising and copy placement decisions; (3) overseeing corrections of both advertising and editorial copy; (4) working closely with advertising department to insure copy approved by client; (5) meeting weekly deadline.

Left when pregnant with second child. Had re-hire status but moved from area due to husband's transfer. Is resuming career after recent divorce.

1963–1964
CHEMICAL ABSTRACTS

As Librarian, gained experience in check-out, return, and records of all foreign language and chemical journals. Left due to marriage and husband's transfer.

1962–1963
OHIO STATE SCHOOL FOR RETARDED

Began as volunteer Junior League project, hired part-time as recreational therapist working with younger children. Established good rapport and achieved excellent results. Program eliminated due to financial cut-backs.

MISCELLANEOUS

During homemaker hiatus, has continued interest in children welfare volunteering as teacher aide. Also writes, types and edits newsletters for Parent Teacher Association and various Junior League brochures and releases.

REFERENCES

Available

Synopsis of Resume of:
LORETTA WILKINSON

9778 Hickman Rd.
Des Moines, IA 50322
Phone: (515) 281–8596

.JOB OBJECTIVE

Medical field combined with general office. Job interest more important than salary.

EDUCATION

1950–1952	Drake University, Des Moines, Iowa.
1978	Pine Shores Hospital, Kansas City, Mo. Completed Ward Clerk Course. 435 hours.
Skills:	Typing, speedwriting, adding machine, calculator. Familiarity with medical terminology.

EXPERIENCE '

1970–1975	INTERNAL REVENUE SERVICE, Kansas City, Missouri Secretary to Chief.
Prior	IOWA-DES MOINES NAT. BANK, Des Moines, Iowa. Secretary to Vice-President.
	GENERAL HOSPITAL, Des Moines, Iowa. Volunteer hospital work in varied capacities.

PERSONAL

Born:	1930; widow; excellent health. Height 5'; wt. 105 lbs.
Finances:	Good order; owns home, car, income property.
Hobbies:	Tennis; crossword puzzles; genealogy research.
Affiliations:	St. Andrews Society; Brentwood Country Club.

(FOR AMPLIFICATION SEE FOLLOWING)

Financially independent "displaced homemaker" who has been gainfully employed in earlier years and wishes to re-enter job market in other than volunteer capacity, conveyed by objective's "job interest." No-date "career highlights" point up capabilities while soft pedaling homemaking years.

Amplified Resume   Loretta Wilkinson - page 2

CAREER HIGHLIGHTS

Iowa-Des Moines National Bank

Immediately following college, employed as secretary to vice-president. Performed standard secretarial functions; dictation, typing, bookkeeping, and filing, utilizing and honing basic skills acquired during part-time stenographic jobs during high school. Left for marriage.

Internal Revenue Service, Kansas City, Missouri

With family raised, took job as secretary to Chief, Field Audit for the State of Missouri. Took dictation, typed letters, received visitors, received and sorted mail. Kept time and attendance reports for 100 personnel, as well as statutory period of limitation control cards. Left in 1975 due to husband's illness and returned to Des Moines.

Transcon Industries

Working out of home, became local distributor for Transcon Industries. Bought the costume jewelry ring distributorship, serviced boutiques, beauty shops, drug stores and dress shops. Succeeded in establishing 25 lucrative accounts before company went out of business.

Miscellaneous

Volunteer work in hospitals, and Ward Clerk Course afforded experience and knowledge in:
  Maintaining patient charts and records.
  Transcribing doctors' orders for medical records.
  Programming patient medications, tests, and diets.
  Ordering supplies, blood and drugs from hospital pharmacist.
  Graphing vital statistics for nurses; receiving patients.
  Maintaining costs incurred for patient treatment.

REFERENCES

On Request